The Honour of God's Name

The Honour of God's Name

Do our thoughts and actions match our prayers?

Graham Criddle

Copyright © Graham Criddle, 2024

All rights reserved. No part of this book may be reproduced or transmitted in any form or by any means, electronic or mechanical, including photocopying, recording, or by any information storage and retrieval system, without permission in writing from the author.

Acknowledgments

I want to thank Jo, my wife, who encouraged me in writing this book – including me spending quite a bit of time on a holiday some years ago doing some of the early planning around content and structure!

I also want to thank my two sons, Richard and David, who commented on early drafts of this book and provided helpful insights and perspectives. The final content of the book, and any errors or omissions, are mine.

I am also grateful to the community at Gold Hill Baptist Church who invited me to speak at a seminar on this topic, providing the opportunity to explore in more detail some of the ideas and principles.

Table of Contents

INTRODUCTION 1

ANY FORM OF IDOLATRY IS NOT OK 10

DISOBEDIENCE HAS CONSEQUENCES 29

LEADERS GETTING IT WRONG 35

THE FOCUS ON DEFENDING THE HONOUR OF GOD'S NAME................43

THE GLORY OF GOD 51

GOD IS "THE LORD" 60

IMPLICATIONS FOR US 73

BIBLIOGRAPHY 85

Introduction

The "Lord's Prayer" or "the prayer that Jesus taught his disciples" is probably the most well-known prayers in the Bible. It's found in Matthew 6:9-13 (or a slightly reduced form in Luke 11:2-4). It is seen as a model for Christian prayer as it encourages followers of Jesus to regularly affirm our relationship with God, to recognise who God is, to pray for his purposes to be fulfilled, to pray for the help and support we need.

It has been prayed by the church for centuries and is prayed regularly by hundreds of millions of Christians every day – privately and in many different forms of church services.

But does our familiarity with it carry the risk of not really focusing on what we are praying, of not understanding the power of what Jesus was calling for? In Matthew, this prayer appears in the Sermon on the Mount which is a block of teaching calling for radical transformation in the lives of his followers. It is not unreasonable to expect that the words of the prayer carry with it some expectation of radical change as well. Maybe it is not enough that we pray this prayer, but that the guiding driver in our lives is to help it become a reality.

Hallowed be your name

The phrase from that prayer that was the reason I wrote this book (found in Matthew 6:9) has been translated in a variety of ways:

- hallowed be your name (NIV)
- may your name be kept holy (NLT)
- may your name be honored (NET)

What does it mean be something to be "hallowed", how can God's name be kept holy, how can it be honoured? Is it something that only God can do (after all it is included in a prayer to God) or is it something that requires action on the part of God's people for the prayer to be answered?

Various ideas as to what it entails have been suggested:

- This prayer is not so much a petition that God will do some great act that will show everyone who and what he is, as a prayer that he will bring people to a proper attitude toward him. It expresses an aspiration that he who is holy will be seen to be holy and treated throughout his creation as holy.[1]
- "Name" refers to one's person, character, and authority. All that God stands for should be treated as holy and honored because of his utter perfection and goodness.[2]
- the hallowing of God's name, the acceptance of his kingship and the doing of his will involve human response (including that of the ones praying)[3]
- Therefore to pray that God's "name" be "hallowed"[4] is not to pray that God may become holy but that he may be treated as holy (cf. Exod 20:8; Lev 19:2, 32; Ezek 36:23; 1 Peter 1:15), that his name should not be despised (Mal 1:6) by the thoughts and conduct of those who have been created in his image.[5]
- This is, in fact, a prayer for the kingdom of God to become fully present: not for God's people to be snatched away from earth to heaven, but for the glory and beauty of heaven to be turned into earthly reality as well. When that is done, God's name—his character, his reputation, his very presence—will be held in high honour everywhere[6]

---

[1] Leon Morris, *The Gospel according to Matthew*, The Pillar New Testament Commentary (Grand Rapids, MI; Leicester, England: W.B. Eerdmans; Inter-Varsity Press, 1992), 145.

[2] Craig Blomberg, *Matthew*, vol. 22, The New American Commentary (Nashville: Broadman & Holman Publishers, 1992), 119.

[3] R. T. France, *The Gospel of Matthew*, The New International Commentary on the New Testament (Grand Rapids, MI: Wm. B. Eerdmans Publication Co., 2007), 246.

[4] the verbal form of "holy," recurring in Matt only at 23:17, 19 [NIV, "makes sacred"]

[5] D. A. Carson, "Matthew," in *The Expositor's Bible Commentary: Matthew, Mark, Luke*, ed. Frank E. Gaebelein, vol. 8 (Grand Rapids, MI: Zondervan Publishing House, 1984), 170.

[6] Tom Wright, *Matthew for Everyone, Part 1: Chapters 1-15* (London: Society for Promoting Christian Knowledge, 2004), 59.

There is clearly a sense of calling on God to act, but implicit in that is the call on God's people to act in a way that aligns ourselves with this purpose. And if we don't get this right, then the rest of the prayer – about God's kingdom coming, about God's will being done, on the things that we need, of confession and forgiveness – lose much, if not all, of their meaning.

This raises the question of how we, as individuals and as communities of believers, engage with this phrase and with the prayer as a whole.

- Is it something we rarely read, say or think about?
- Is it something that is a regular component in our worship?
- And, if so, has it become ritual or does it continue to be fresh and a key part of our ongoing relationship with God?

What does the phrase – about God's name being hallowed or kept holy, mean to you? Is it something you are praying that God will do and leaving it all up to him, or do you recognise that praying these words meaningfully have consequences for who we are and how we live?

Purpose and focus of this book – why Ezekiel?

The purpose and focus of this book is to explore this phrase within the prayer – the call for God's name to be kept holy, be hallowed, be honoured. And it does this by examining a range of passages in the Old Testament book of Ezekiel. On the face of it, this might be a strange place to start as there are other options available such as focusing on another book, such as Exodus; or reviewing the entirety of the Old Testament for what it says about this theme.[7]

So why the focus on Ezekiel?

---

[7] That would be a different type of book – and much longer!

For any not familiar with the book, it is an account of visions, and some associated activities, that were given to a young man called Ezekiel. He was a 30-year-old priest when his prophetic ministry started (Ezekiel 1:1) by which time he was among a group of Jews who had been taken away as exiles into Babylon in 597BC as God's punishment for their ongoing disobedience. While Ezekiel's visions were given to him in Babylon, most of them focused on what was going on back in Jerusalem, commenting on those events and looking forward to how God was going to bring the exile to an end. It was a challenging and turbulent time for people such as Ezekiel and the visions he was given would have helped to explain what was going on, would have challenged behaviour and would have given hope for the future.

Reading through Ezekiel on one occasion, I was struck by the repeated occasions where God acts to defend the honour of his name, to force people to recognise that he is Lord, to acknowledge that his authority is supreme. The clear message of the book is that God's actions – even towards his own chosen people – are not primarily to bless his people but to protect his own name and reputation. This might be very strange, and slightly disturbing, to us today as we often seem to expect God to bless us as one of his primary functions. So this book, among other things, seeks to provide a corrective to such mis-expectations we might have.

If we were to examine one of the earlier books and see what it says about God's name, we would find out something about the importance God places on his name. So Exodus, for example, has God speaking about his name five times:

- In Exodus 3:15, God tells Moses to tell the people of Israel about his name
- In Exodus 6:3, God explains that the patriarchs did not know him by his name as **The Lord**
- In Exodus 9:16, God makes clear that through the plagues he was going to bring on Egypt, his name was going to be honoured throughout the earth
- In Exodus 20:24, God speaks about honouring his name and blessing his people
- In Exodus 33:19. God speaks about appearing to Moses and proclaiming his name to him

These are all passages that tell us something about the way in which God views his name and the honour to be associated with it. But they do not address the issues that arise when God's name is not honoured as it should be. That is something that only becomes apparent over time as the people of God turn away from him. So, to examine this theme it is more appropriate to study one of the later prophetic books as the prophet speaks out God's word against the failures of his people. These, in turn, can encourage us today to examine our attitudes and practices to see if we are falling into similar behaviour and not giving God's name the honour it deserves.

The two main contenders, in terms of focus on this particular theme, are Jeremiah and Ezekiel.[8] Jeremiah is written before the exile warning about the consequences of not honouring God, while Ezekiel is written during the exile that happened as a result of not doing so. Of the two, I've chosen to focus on Ezekiel as it was "nearer" to the time when Jesus was on earth and encouraging his followers to pray that God's name be hallowed. They would have been able to look back on all the experiences of the past, and the things that God's people had learnt, to gain a deeper insight into what hallowing God's name really meant.

Hundreds of years after the time of Ezekiel, as Jesus presents his model prayer, the reality of the exile and what happened after the return from exile would have been very real in the shared memory of the people. And the insights from Ezekiel's story could have helped them, can help us, understand something of the importance that God attaches to the integrity of his name and the actions he takes to defend it. The story of Ezekiel also speaks about many things the people of God did that sadly brought God's name into disrepute, things that we are still able to do – even if in different ways – today. His story challenges us regarding our actions and to consider whether they are consistent with this phrase that we are called to pray. And, if not, his story challenges us to change how we live in order so that God's name can indeed be honoured.

---

[8] Jeremiah has God speaking about his name 22 times while there are 14 occurrences in Ezekiel.

One of the things that really challenged me in reading through Ezekiel was those occasions where God's chosen people are accused by God of profaning or defiling his name (see Ezekiel 20:9-39; 36:20-23; 39:7; 43:7-8) and the different ways in which they did it. What a terrible indictment. How far the people had come from the relationship God had called them into. And as we look deeper into Ezekiel, we see that right from the beginning of the relationship God had with his people, they were acting in ways that dishonoured him. Another powerful theme that keeps on repeating is that of God wanting people to recognise that he is the Lord and this desire causing God to act, to punish, to protect. The over-riding message is that God acts time and time again in order to protect his name, for people to recognise that he is sovereign.

This should cause us to stop and think about our understanding of God and his actions: how much do we expect God to act in a way that blesses us and how much do we expect God to act in a way that brings honour to him? Are our expectations correct or have we lost a godly perspective on life?

Structure of the book

This book, then, looks at this significant phrase about God's name being honoured near the beginning of this model prayer and reflects on it by examining some of the events in the book of Ezekiel. It does this in two main sections, with a bridging chapter between them:

1. The first section looks at the actions of God's people that brought his name into disrepute
2. Then there is a bridging chapter that explores why honouring God's name is seen as so important
3. The second section looks at a couple of things that are important to God and helps us understand why he acts in the way he does
4. Then there is a final chapter that encourages us to reflect on the things learned from the book of Ezekiel and to see what it has to say to us today as we live as God's people and pray that God's name be honoured.

There are clearly overlaps between the two sections as, in both, God and his people are acting and reacting with each other. The major theme that ties them together – and that is explored in the bridging chapter - is the importance that God places on his name. If God did not place such honour on his name, then the failings of his people would not have been as significant and the need to act to defend it would have been reduced. As we explore the failings of God's people and his response to that; as we see something of the importance God places on the honour of his name; we will gain a deeper insight into what we are really praying when we ask that God's name be kept holy, and we will be challenged regarding whether our attitudes and actions are contributing towards this.

The first major section looks at some of the actions of God's people that brought dishonour to God and how God responded:

- The first chapter in this section shows that the major issue was that of idolatry – giving something else the worship that God alone deserves. This presented itself in many different ways, carried out by many different types of people, reminding us that idolatry today can appear in many different forms some of which we may not be recognise
- The second chapter examines some of the consequence of disobeying God's law
- The last chapter in this section looks at the problem of people in authority acting against God's law and leading his people astray

The second section examines two of the key themes that thread through the book of Ezekiel, highlighting some of the things that are presented as being important to God:

- The first chapter in this section looks at how the book recognises the glory of God
- The second chapter in this section looks at the sovereignty of God

When these are challenged or disregarded, God's name is not being honoured and these chapters explore different ways in which God acts when his name and reputation have been damaged and will do many things to restore that reputation.

To help understand the importance attached to God's name, it is important to know how names were seen in Old Testament times. Today, in many cultures, they are effectively seen as labels, as a way of identifying someone or something. In Old Testament times, however, they had a much deeper significance and were thought to describe the person or the thing they related to. Moses, for example, was so named as he had been "drawn out of the water" (Exodus 2:10).[9] So all through his life he would have been reminded of where he had come from (and it may well have resulted in some interesting questions and conversations!).

So with God being ultimately and uniquely holy, his name needed to be treated as such. If not, it raised questions as to the very character and nature of God. And so God would act to defend the honour of his name as it spoke about who he was. This would cause difficulty and hardship for his people if they had contributed towards his loss of honour. Because, as we will see, God's priority is not to give his people an easy life but to maintain his reputation.

A modern-day parallel, though with much lesser impact, would be inappropriate behaviour of professional sports people whose actions impacts how the whole team is perceived. Often the managers of those teams need to impose discipline on those who have offended and make statements saying that the actions of these players were inconsistent with the standards expected of them. Wrong actions have impacts, they damage reputations, resulting in action needing to be taken to restore the standing of the team. And, at that point, the standing of the team takes priority over how the disciplinary action will impact the individuals involved – they have brought the team into disrepute, they need to accept the consequences.

When we pray that God's name is honoured, we are calling on God to act to defend his name and this might be dangerous for us if we are not living in ways that contribute towards that honour. This can result in different responses two of which are suggested below:

1. That we stop praying this phrase as we don't want our sinful lifestyles to be challenged or changed

---

[9] In Hebrew, the name sounds similar to the verb that means "draw out".

2. That we commit to living in ways that honour God, making it possible for us to continue to pray this phrase and really mean it

The final chapter of the book brings some of these ideas together and suggests ways in which we can live in order to uphold the honour of God's name.

As outlined above, in each section we will be looking at different parts of Ezekiel to see what it tells us about God, about his name, and how he acts to protect it. We will also look at a range of different Bible passages that add further depth and insight. Please have a Bible with you when working through this book so you can look up and read the different passages mentioned - some of the key passages will be reproduced in this book. And if you haven't read Ezekiel before, or haven't looked at it for some time, it would be a good idea to read it through before continuing in this book to get an overall sense of what is going on and what it says.

As we take time to reflect on this important phrase through the lens of Ezekiel, let's keep in mind the importance God places on the honour of his name and let's think about whether our actions need to change in order to honour him more.

Any form of idolatry is not OK

Idolatry is about people worshiping something other than the God who alone deserved it, and who expected it from his people. As such, it draws attention and focus away from God, putting other things in his place. It says that other things can be put alongside God as recipients of worship and this suggests that God is not unique, is not separate, is not holy. As such it is totally incompatible with maintaining the honour of God's name.

We will see, during this section, that God's people in Ezekiel failed in all these, and other, ways and so were being punished for their attitude and actions towards God and his name.

God makes it clear that idolatry is totally unacceptable when he gives the 10 Commandments to his people, with these appearing as the first two:

3 'You shall have no other gods before me. 4 'You shall not make for yourself an image in the form of anything in heaven above or on the earth beneath or in the waters below. 5 You shall not bow down to them or worship them; for I, the LORD your God, am a jealous God, punishing the children for the sin of the parents to the third and fourth generation of those who hate me, 6 but showing love to a thousand generations of those who love me and keep my commandments. (Exodus 20:3-6).[10]

It is clear, it is important, breaking this brings consequences.

But hundreds of years later, the people of God are accused of having broken this cardinal commandment in different ways and, through that, bringing dishonour onto God's name. In response, God acts to restore his standing in the sight of his people and those observing their actions.

---

[10] The third commandment, about not misusing God's name, will be picked up later.

One of the things we will see as we look through Ezekiel, is that the practice of idolatry can take place in many different ways and at different levels in society. The specifics are different, but the underlying sin is the same. It is presented as something that angers and pains God, something that damages relationship with him, something that results in punishment, something that can impact others. It is something that (maybe after a long time) results in punishment, it is something that can have severe and long-term consequences for groups and for individuals. The accounts in Ezekiel challenge us to think of our own lives and practices and to consider whether there is anything idolatrous in them at all. If so, it is painful to God and something we should seek to remove and have nothing further to do with.

Idolatry - a chronic condition (Ezekiel 20)

One of the things that Ezekiel makes clear is that this problem of idolatry had been around for a very long time. It was a type of behaviour that the people had failed to shake off, and showed little indication of wanting to do so. And as the story is told, we have reason to be amazed that God waited so long to bring punishment on his people. A real demonstration of mercy – not treating people as they deserved – but, eventually, judgment fell.

The story is laid out in Ezekiel 20 and asks important questions about the basis of the relationship between God and the people he had chosen.

It starts back in Egypt where the people had been reduced to slavery and had been in bondage for hundreds of years. God acts powerfully, through Moses and Aaron and via the use of 10 plagues, to rescue his people and bring them out towards the land he had promised them. But it is shocking to see that, even when in Egypt, the people had been worshipping the gods of their Egyptian masters.

⁴ 'Will you judge them? Will you judge them, son of man? Then confront them with the detestable practices of their ancestors ⁵ and say to them: "This is what the Sovereign LORD says: on the day I chose Israel, I swore with uplifted hand to the descendants of Jacob and revealed myself to them in Egypt. With uplifted hand I said to them, 'I am the LORD your God.' ⁶ On that day I swore to them that I would bring them out of Egypt into a land I had searched out for them, a land flowing with milk and honey, the most beautiful of all lands. ⁷ And I said to them, 'Each of you, get rid of the vile images you have set your eyes on, and do not defile yourselves with the idols of Egypt. I am the LORD your God.' (Ezekiel 20:4-7).

Some of the elders of Israel had just come to Ezekiel, hoping that he could share some godly wisdom into what was going on, as to why they were in this situation. But God responds by calling the prophet to challenge them about how their ancestors had behaved hundreds of years before and ever since. The reason for raising this is to challenge them as to whether they were going to continue to behave in the same way.

God's point is that on the day he appeared to them in Egypt, on the day he said he was going to rescue them, he called on them to get rid of the images and idols of Egypt that had become so important to them. God was staking his claim to be their God, he was calling on them to get rid of anything that would interfere in that relationship.

On the face of it, this is an easy decision for the people to make. They had been held captives for hundreds of years, the God who had revealed himself to their founding fathers had suddenly appeared to them again and had renewed his promises of blessing. He had promised to bring them out of slavery and into a land of plenty that he had chosen for them. In response, he was looking for them to get rid of the idols and images that had not done anything for them, images that would have kept them linked to their time in Egypt as opposed to looking ahead to what God had in store for them.

But, shockingly, they refused.

⁷ And I said to them, 'Each of you, get rid of the vile images you have set your eyes on, and do not defile yourselves with the idols of Egypt. I am the LORD your God.' ⁸ ' "But they rebelled against me and would not listen to me; they did not get rid of the vile images they had set their eyes on, nor did they forsake the idols of Egypt. So I said I would pour out my wrath on them and spend my anger against them in Egypt. (Ezekiel 20:7-8).

The language is powerful and clear.

It was not just a command to the leaders of the people but to each and every one of them. They were all engaged in worshipping idols and they each were being called on to decide to stop, to get rid of them, to focus on God.

These images were described as vile, things that would defile the people, things that had no place among them. But the people refused, they rebelled and chose to hold on to them – even as the God who was going to redeem them commanded them to get rid of them.

No wonder, God's intention was to be angry and to punish them while they were still in Egypt. Why should he bring them out if they refused to listen, if they weren't prepared to relate to him as they should?

But then we get the sense of a change in God's plans, he is not going to punish them, but he is going to bring them out of bondage after all. And the reason for the change is that God wanted to defend the honour of his name.

9 But for the sake of my name, I brought them out of Egypt. I did it to keep my name from being profaned in the eyes of the nations among whom they lived and in whose sight I had revealed myself to the Israelites. (Ezekiel 20:9).

Even though they were unwilling to get rid of the idols that would impede their worship of God, even though this caused God to be angry, God chose to not punish them but to continue in his plan for rescue. God had promised to rescue them and, if he hadn't it would have looked as though he was unable to. So even though, even while still in Egypt, they were rebellious and idolatrous God rescued them because he had said he would. Nothing about them deserving it - they did not - but it was to protect the honour of God's name.

This casts light on the events surrounding the tenth and final plague as God prepared to pass through the land of Egypt and cause all the firstborn to die. It wasn't just the people of Egypt who were in danger, but the people of Israel as well, requiring them to paint the blood of a lamb on the doorposts of their houses to keep the destroying angel outside (Exodus 12:7,13). The judgment of God was going to fall on 'all the gods of Egypt' (Exodus 20:12) and, if these gods were present in the homes and lives of God's people, they also needed to be protected from that punishment.[11]

This early and deep-rooted presence of idols among the people in Egypt was not just an issue at that time, but it also helps to explain why idol worship keeps coming up in the story of Israel:

- Those first two commandments that we mentioned earlier (Exodus 20:3-6) were not just to prevent against something that might happen in the future but to break the habits of lifetimes and generations.
- The golden calf that Aaron made for the people as they were concerned that Moses had left them (Exodus 32:1-6) was not a new concept to them, but a return to practices they should have left behind. And Ezekiel reminds the elders of this as he speaks about how their ancestors rebelled against God in the wilderness (Exodus 20:13).
- The warnings Moses gave to the people as they prepared to enter the Promised Land regarding the consequences of worshipping foreign gods (Deuteronomy 29:25-28) were a stark reminder of the importance of worshipping God alone.
- Joshua – towards the end of his life – reminds the people of the time they worshipped foreign gods (Joshua 24:15) and has to command them to get rid of the idols that were still among them (Joshua 24:23) making it clear that their presence and influence was still very real, a temptation to turn back to what should have been in their past and to turn away from worshipping God. So parents had passed on idols to their children who still preserved them just as Ezekiel reminds them (Ezekiel 20:21).
- It was a recurring theme in the book of Judges, with a cycle of the people turning away from God and worshipping idols, God punishing them, the people crying out for help and God raising up judges to rescue them (Judges 2:10-19). This practice is referred to by Ezekiel as he speaks about the constant practice of worshipping foreign gods and causing God to be angry (Ezekiel 20:28).
- Even the kings of the nation worshipped foreign gods and led the people astray, with one of the worst examples being

---

[11] John MacArthur and Richard Mayhue, eds., *Biblical Doctrine: A Systematic Summary of Bible Truth* (Wheaton, IL: Crossway, 2017), 310.

Manasseh who even placed the carved image of a god in God's Temple (2 Kings 21:7).

It was not a theoretical issue that needed to be warned against but something that was very real in their society, something that was there from the time the nation was born until the time that God sent them into exile, as he had promised he would do (Deuteronomy 28:58-64).

They seemed to have a 'natural tendency to idolatry' and continued to fall back into these patterns of life and worship. They did not get rid of the idols their ancestors had revered but continued to give them place in their lives.[12]

We are left wondering why God put up with this wicked behaviour for so long and it seems to be primarily due to God's desire to preserve the honour of his name, a repeated theme in Ezekiel 20.

- He did not destroy them in Egypt but brought them out for the sake of his name and to keep his name from being profaned (Ezekiel 20:9)
- He continued to not punish them through their wilderness journeys so his name and reputation would not suffer in the sight of the surrounding nations (Ezekiel 20:14)
- This forbearance continued through into the second generation of people even though they continued to disobey and to focus on idols (Ezekiel 20:22-24)

It is also true that it was God's love for his people that caused him to hold back on judgment for so long, as Greenberg points out:

> Rashi comments: "God evidently suppressed his resentment over it for close to 900 years—from the time they were in Egypt to Ezekiel's day—overmastered by his love toward the people. But it reawakened because of their excessive sinfulness, illustrating the proverb 'Hatred wakens quarrels, but love covers all offenses' (Prov 10:12)" (based on *Leviticus Rabba* 7.1).[13]

---

[12] D. T. Bernard, "Ezekiel on the Early History of Religion in Israel.—Ch. 20," *The Churchman* 17, no. 1–12 (1902–1903): 228.
[13] Moshe Greenberg, *Ezekiel 1–20: A New Translation with Introduction and Commentary*, vol. 22, Anchor Yale Bible (New Haven; London: Yale University Press, 2008), 365.

But the clear sense from Ezekiel is that the primary driver is God's desire to preserve the honour of his name and to not allow the disobedient practices of his people to bring it into disrepute. What a terrible indictment of God's people, that their actions were likely to dishonour God, causing him to have to act to prevent that happening.

So, Ezekiel 20 makes it clear that worshipping of foreign gods had been present in the lives of God's people for centuries. It had not stopped God rescuing them from Egypt or keeping them safe through the wilderness. But it had angered God and, eventually, resulted in him acting to defend the honour of his name even though that meant sending his people into exile.

It looks as though the exile was successful in ridding idol-worship from God's people with very little reference to it in the post-exilic writings. Gleason goes so far as to say:

> The terrible ordeal of the Babylonian captivity had brought about a complete rejection of graven images on the part of the Jewish remnant[14]

He points out that the post-exilic authors have nothing to say about idolatry being a problem and so concludes that it was a thing of the past as far as God's people were concerned.[15] (Some argue[16] that the reference to a foreign god in Malachi 2:11 does speak about a problem with idol worship but, even if that is the case, it does seem to be an isolated incident).

In fact, effort seems to be taken to avoid any possibility of idolatry returning to the land with Nehemiah acting against men who had married foreign wives (Nehemiah 13:23-28), presumably due to concern over them possibly bringing idol worship with them into the home and the community.

And when a Greek king, Antiochus IV Epiphanes, seeks to impose Greek practices on the people in Jerusalem including setting up an idol in the temple it caused a revolt as people fought a bitter war to reverse this practice.[17]

---

[14] Gleason Archer Jr., *A Survey of Old Testament Introduction*, 3rd. ed. (Chicago: Moody Press, 1994), 378.

[15] Gleason Archer Jr., *A Survey of Old Testament Introduction*, 3rd. ed. (Chicago: Moody Press, 1994), 379.

[16] See, for example, the discussion in Ralph L. Smith, *Micah–Malachi*, vol. 32, Word Biblical Commentary (Dallas: Word, Incorporated, 1984), 321

The experience of exile seemed to have achieved one of its purposes in curing the people of idolatry – one of the major causes of God's name being dishonoured.

But that is all in the future. At the time of Ezekiel, it was not just that idolatry had been a problem in the past but that it was a very current problem even as the exile was in progress. Ezekiel 8 gives some examples of the evil practices that caused God to become angry and we turn to that next. But before we move onto that next section, it's important to pause and consider what contemporary implications we can draw from what we have seen.

Where do we find chronic idolatry today?

We have seen that for hundreds of years there had been a tension between God and his people, a tension that was at the heart of the relationship that God had intended for them. That instead of being completely and totally devoted to God and worshipping only him the people, and often their leaders, continued to return to false gods and idolatry.

We get the sense that the people were secure in their standing as God's people and trusting in the promises that he had made regarding land, prosperity and security and had forgotten their responsibilities towards him. And for centuries they had continued to live in confident safety – even through various ups and downs and a gradual erosion of their position in the world. It had got to the point where, with occasional exceptions, the worship of God was carried on side-by-side with following idols. For many people this would have been what they were brought up to think was normal, they would have had no idea that anything was wrong. And this continued until that moment when God acted to defend the honour of his name and sent his people into exile.

---

[17] Daniel J. Harrington, "Antiochus," ed. David Noel Freedman, Allen C. Myers, and Astrid B. Beck, *Eerdmans Dictionary of the Bible* (Grand Rapids, MI: W.B. Eerdmans, 2000), 69.

The question it raises for us is whether anything similar is going on today. This could be in our own lives and our individual focus of worship and devotion; it could be in our individual churches; it could be in the church traditions that we are part of.

Such practices may have been with us for centuries in our church traditions, for generations in our churches, for decades in our families. They may seem normal, they may seem right, we may not see that they are not faithful and honouring to God. But they are forms of idolatry, grieve God and take away the honour that he alone deserves.

I saw an example of this when visiting a church abroad, a church that had been established by missionaries from a foreign country fifty years earlier. And to honour those missionaries, the way the church operated, and the way services were organised, were exactly as they have been set up half a century earlier. The fact that it had little relationship to their cultural context and no thought for God wanting to do new things among them did not seem to cause any concern at all. And, nearer to home, we don't need to look too closely to find similar examples in church life and practice – even to the extent of it being virtually impossible to change the time of a service or get rid of a musical instrument that is no longer used.

As we reflect on the historical practices of God's people, it is vitally important that we examine ourselves and are prepared to ask the hard questions as to whether we are doing something similar. And if so, to seek God's forgiveness and to move back into a closer relationship with him and with him alone. As we do so, we follow the example of Daniel who, as exile drew to a close, was prepared to come to God and to confess his sin and the sins of his people and ask God to restore his people for the honour of his name (Daniel 9:1-29).

A deeply resistant problem (Ezekiel 8)

It seems nearly beyond belief to recognise that the practice of idolatry continued back in Jerusalem even after many of its inhabitants had been taken away into exile in Babylon because of their idolatry. But this is what Ezekiel becomes aware of as he is transported back to Jerusalem in a vision (Ezekiel 8:4).

As we read through the chapter, we see that this is affecting many different parts of society – with some of it becoming carried out in plain view of everyone while some of it is being done in private. But whether public or private, not even the impact of their fellow Israelites being carried away into exile has caused this practice to stop. Maybe there was a feeling that the gods of the Babylonians had won and were to be worshipped, maybe it was so ingrained by this time that even those traumatic events were insufficient to change people's behaviour.

Rivals to worship

The first indication that idol worship continues to be a problem is the 'idol that provokes jealousy' (Ezekiel 8:3) standing in the temple, the place that should have been totally given over to the worship of God alone.

As one went further and further into the temple, the things that occupied worshippers in their daily lives were to be left behind and their thoughts and attention were to turn towards God. But the presence of this statue would have interrupted their focus and drawn their thoughts away from God again.

For it to be within the temple itself, it must have received the approval of those responsible for the maintenance of the temple and the conduct of worship there. It has been suggested[18] that this was the idol that had been set up by Manasseh (2 Chronicles 33:7) but, wherever it had come from, it was an affront to God and would have detracted from the worship he deserved.

As Block points out, the statement that this idol provoked jealousy was a direct reference to the impact that the presence of this idol had on God as it challenged his position of supreme authority and only valid focus of worship.[19] It went directly against a clear command he had given to his people hundreds of years previously where he had made clear his jealous feelings towards them (Deuteronomy 4:15-31).

---

[18] Lamar Eugene Cooper, *Ezekiel*, vol. 17, The New American Commentary (Nashville: Broadman & Holman Publishers, 1994), 120.

[19] Daniel Isaac Block, *The Book of Ezekiel, Chapters 1–24*, The New International Commentary on the Old Testament (Grand Rapids, MI: Wm. B. Eerdmans Publishing Co., 1997), 282.

But even as Ezekiel sees this image in his vision, he is confronted with the pure and magnificent glory of God (Ezekiel 8:4), in contrast to the inert, fixed, presence of the idol. It is as though there is a contest here between God and this idol; not a contest about position or supremacy or power as that is not in dispute, but a contest for the hearts and minds of God's people. As we look further we see that this is a real contest with the people doing many things that would drive God away from the place he had chosen to dwell among his people (Ezekiel 8:6). And a little later we see the glory of God leaving the temple and the city (Ezekiel 10:4, 18, 19; 11:23) as though the continuing practice of idol worship had become too much for God to accept. Not only had he sent his people into exile, but he was choosing to exile himself. But there is the wonderful promise that this is not how the story will end: God will bring his people back, God will return and the relationship will be restored (Ezekiel 11:14-21).

But that is in the (near) future. The rest of Ezekiel 8 shows us some of the things that were taking place that grieved God to the point where he would leave his temple and city. Each one is presented as something that is worse than the one before, as we see a growing attack on a right relationship to God and towards worship.

Leaders caught in compromising situations

God commands Ezekiel to dig through one of the walls of the temple court and, as he does so he sees a doorway. On opening the door, he sees pictures of unclean objects on the wall and the images that were used for idol worship in Israel. Shockingly worse, he sees that those who are in the room and worshipping these idols were 'seventy elders of Israel' and a man called Jaazaniah (Ezekiel 8:7-11). The censers provide clear proof that their reason for being there is to worship these images and they seem to believe that they are safe doing so because God cannot see them, because God has deserted them. It has even got to the point that each of them has their own idol instead of them all being united in their worship of God (Ezekiel 8:12).

One could argue that at least they are doing this in secret. They are not, at least as far as this account goes, engaging in public idolatry that could lead others astray. But that is not the point. When the leaders of God's people are not living as they should, are not focusing on God as they should, are not letting God have the first place that he demands and deserves; then they will not be honouring God, they are unable to lead God's people aright.

Crying out to a foreign god

With an idolatrous image set up in the temple, with their leaders engaged in idolatrous practices, it is no surprise to see the ordinary people having their focus turned away from God and engaging with idols and false gods.

The first instance we see of this is women 'mourning the god Tammuz' (Ezekiel 8:14).

No explanation is given here but as we look into what was happening it becomes clear that these women had lost their confidence in God to provide for them.

Tammuz was the Babylonian god of vegetation and when vegetation died during the late summer and winter months, women engaged in a rite of crying for Tammuz as though he, himself, had died. And then, there was rejoicing in the spring when vegetation sprang to life again and the resurrection of this god was celebrated.[20]

So what these women were doing in the temple was engaging in this practice, thereby acknowledging that these foreign gods were responsible for the cycle of nature – as opposed to the God of Israel who had demonstrated his power in creation. They were blatantly and openly recognising their dependence on someone other than God. Instead of worshipping God, they were mourning the death of an imaginary idol.[21] The fact that they were doing it in the temple either meant that, in their minds, they had totally replaced the worship of God with these idols or that they were integrating various cultic rituals into their worship. Either of these had been expressly forbidden by God for his people.

---

[20] Lamar Eugene Cooper, *Ezekiel*, vol. 17, The New American Commentary (Nashville: Broadman & Holman Publishers, 1994), 123.

Nature being exalted above its creator

Finally on his journey, Ezekiel reaches the inner court of the temple and finds 25 men worshipping the sun (Ezekiel 8:16-18). The symbology is clear and powerful – they have turned away from the temple of God and turned towards the sun as an object of worship; the sun that God had created and placed in the sky (Genesis 1:16-17). This type of practice had been explicitly prohibited by God and carried with it the death penalty as a way of removing evil from among the people (Deuteronomy 17:1-7). But here it was taking place openly in the inner court of the temple.

There was no hiding how far the people of God had fallen. The presence of public idols, the practice of private idolatry, the incorporation of foreign rituals, the worship of elements in the natural world – all of these pointed to a people who were far away from God and his purposes for them.

A sad and terrible state of affairs that clearly grieved God deeply. No wonder he was going to 'deal with them in anger' and ignore their cries to him as things got hard for them (Ezekiel 8:18). God was only going to put up with so much, he would act to defend and restore the honour of his name.

Are our leaders falling short?

This chapter raises questions for those responsible for leading God's people today, those responsible for looking after places of worship.

---

[21] Daniel Isaac Block, *The Book of Ezekiel, Chapters 1–24*, The New International Commentary on the Old Testament (Grand Rapids, MI: Wm. B. Eerdmans Publishing Co., 1997), 296.

Are there things they are doing that continue to provoke God to jealousy, are there things they are doing that cause their congregations to be drawn away from a single-hearted focus on God? As people walk into our buildings, are they encouraged to leave the reality of the world behind for a short time and to enjoy the privilege of being in God's presence and worshipping him, or are there things they see and experience that make it difficult for them to do so?

What are the private practices of those in leadership of God's people today? Are they those of personal contemplation on God, rejoicing in his presence and giving him the first place in their lives? Or are they those where God does not have that place, where they are devoting themselves to other things and where any semblance of living in relationship with God is reserved for their public duties? While some argue that this separation of private life and public duty is appropriate in politics; it has no place in the lives of God's people, particularly those who are responsible for leading others.

Even if we are continuing to worship God, do we allow worship of, attention to, other influences to creep in and dilute the honour that God alone deserves?

Are there even situations where in places of worship and among the communities of God's people, blatant focus and worship of things other than God has crept in and started to become accepted? And can that focus of worship even be the leaders themselves? If so, there should again be an expectation that God will deal in anger with those who are continuing to dishonour him in such a blatant and public way.

Problems and consequences

One of the problems with idol worship is that is gets in the way of the true worship of God. Another problem with it is that it can result in God taking devastating action – and we get a glimpse of this in Ezekiel 6.

Here, God calls on Ezekiel to "prophesy against the mountains" (Ezekiel 6:2).

Mountains, or high places, were often places of worship for foreign gods. God calls on his people to destroy these places that had been used by people in the land before them (Numbers 33:52) but, instead, from early on we see them carrying out sacrifices at these high places (1 Samuel 9:12). Maybe, initially, there was an excuse for continuing to use these places for worship before the temple was built – with this being given as a reason at the start of Solomon's reign. But Solomon is also criticised for offering sacrifices and burning incense there (1 Kings 3:2-3). Even worse, later on in life, Solomon built a high place for foreign gods and offered sacrifices there (1 Kings 11:7-8). With Solomon only being Israel's third king, there is clear concern that this will become established practice and the worship of God will be diluted by focusing on images, idols and foreign gods. And this continues with some of the subsequent kings building shrines, installing priests and sacrificing there (1 Kings 12:31-32; 2 Kings 16:4; 21:3). This, in turn, caused the people to follow suit (1 Kings 14:23; 22:43; 2 Kings 12:3; 17:9-12). There were one or two notable exceptions to this, such as Hezekiah (2 Kings 18:1-4) and Josiah (2 Kings 23), but the norm was to allow or to encourage worship in these high places, the "mountains of Israel" towards which Ezekiel is called to prophesy.

We get the clear sense that God has had enough of this evil practice that diverted people's minds and hearts away from him, and the action he is going to take, as described in Ezekiel 6:3-7, is terrifying.

- He is going to "bring a sword" against them and to destroy them
- The altars will be destroyed so it will no longer be possible to worship there
- God will kill the worshippers in front of their idols – maybe a symbolic statement that these idols had no power to save or to protect
- God will lay out their bodies in public display before their idols
- He will scatter their bones around the alters – not even allowing them a proper burial
- This will extend to the towns and villages where they live so that the destruction will be complete

Looking back at the words I have just written raises many questions in my mind.

- Is this consistent with my understanding of God, the God who is described as being love?
- How about the promises God had made to care for and protect his people? How is his action here consistent with those?
- Why is God acting in this way now? We have just seen that this type of practice had been going on for a long time, why does it call for such a drastic response now?

We're going to consider these from two different perspectives – how this was consistent with God's character and what he had said to his people centuries before; how the following verses provide further context into what is going on.

What God had said before

There are many times when God makes clear to the people how he expects them to behave and what are the consequences of disobedience. One of these is Deuteronomy 4:15-31.

Firstly, they are warned against making idols or worshipping natural objects and the reason given is that God is 'a consuming fire, a jealous God' (Deuteronomy 4:24). This is followed with a clear statement of the consequences of disobedience in verses 25-31. They will be destroyed; God will scatter them; in those foreign lands they will turn to the idols of the people there and worship them. But, even here, there is a message of hope that if they do turn back to God and are obedient to him, they will find God again and be restored into relationship. And the basis for this is nothing about their behaviour or their worth but simply the character and nature of God – the God who is merciful, the God who will not abandon them, the God who will stay faithful to his covenant.

This does not mean that they can simply do as they choose, it does not mean that God will not punish them if they persist in disobedience, but it does mean that God – whatever is going on – remains faithful to his promises for them.

What God was saying then

The verses immediately following these terrifying statements also give answers to these questions – and they continue to call for a realignment of how we think about God. Starting in Ezekiel 6:7 and then another four times up until Ezekiel 7:4, we see God saying that the reason he is going to act is so that his people will know that he is the Lord.[22]

He makes it clear that he has warned them (as we have just seen) – and that the warnings were to be taken seriously (Ezekiel 6:10), and then explains that the time for warning was over and that the end has come (Ezekiel 7:2-3). He was going to judge them based on what they had done and how they had behaved which is something he had promised to do centuries ago and, only now, was bringing it to pass.

So we are in the presence of a faithful God, one who had warned and called for the people to turn back to him over hundreds of years, one who grieved over how they were behaving, one who had made clear the consequences of ongoing rebellion, and one who – at this time – chose to act.

His purpose in judging was to root out the evil among his people and for them to recognise the wickedness of their actions (Ezekiel 6:9-10). Later in the book we will see promises of restoration with the people enjoying good times 'on the mountains of Israel' (Ezekiel 34:11-16) but, here and now, the message is one of time running out and of judgment.

This shows, in terrifying terms, the way God feels towards those who engage in idolatrous practices of worship instead of being committed completely to him. Solomon, for example, had tried to combine the worship of the God of Israel with idols and false gods; others had simply abandoned the worship of God and turned to idols. But they had all allowed worship of something that was of no value at all to replace the worship that was their birthright and calling. As a consequence, they found out how dreadful it can be to 'fall into the hands of the living God' (Hebrews 10:31).

---

[22] We pick up this particular theme in more detail later on.

Punishment delayed doesn't mean punishment won't come

What the people eventually discovered was that following idols, going after other gods, is directly against honouring God's name and that he will judge people for doing that.

This brings with it a challenge about whether we are allowing anyone or anything to take the place that God alone deserves and requires in our lives.

We may feel that we have been allowing this to happen for such a long time that it can't really be a problem. But what Ezekiel 6 shows us is that while God is long-suffering, there does come a point when he acts in judgment towards his unfaithful and uncommitted people.

If this is not the understanding we have of God, then maybe we need to examine whether our understanding is correct!

When our possessions become our idols

Ezekiel 7:10-21 presents another aspect of idol worship, this time relating to wealth.

The passage starts by speaking about the judgment that is going to come on the wicked with the focus being primarily on those who were involved in buying and selling; but with little thought for God.

It's not that there is anything intrinsically wrong with commerce or having money, but the problem here is how that wealth was perceived and how it was used.

It had led them into sin (Ezekiel 7:19), they had become proud of it and had used it to make 'detestable idols' and 'vile images' (Ezekiel 7:20).

Instead of using what they had to bless others and to honour God, they were using it in a way that was deeply displeasing to him. And, because of that, they will be punished, the wealth they took pride in will be given to others, many of them will die.

All of these things: pride, making images, the associated idolatry were forbidden and drew people away from a focus and dependence on God. And, as in the other areas of idolatry we have looked at, God was going to act in judgment upon them.

Sadly, this is not a new problem, rather it is the continuation of practices that have been present in Israel's past. We have already thought about the moment when the people called on Aaron to make a golden calf where he called them to take off their gold earrings and give them to him (Exodus 32:2). Gideon, one of the judges of Israel, asked the people to give him the earrings they had just won in the battle: he turned them into an ephod which the people worshipped (Judges 8:24-27). Two centuries or so before the time of Ezekiel, Hosea spoke about how the people were sinning to using their silver and gold to make idols for themselves (Hosea 8:4). God's charge against the people is clear – that they had taken the good things he had provided for them and used them to worship false gods (Hosea 2:8). A totally wrong thing to do and one that God was going to punish.

Disobedience has consequences

As we have seen, the issue of idolatry and the offence it caused God was a very real problem in the eyes of God and, consequently, would be for the people of God.

But that is not where it ended, there was more – with one of these further issues being the problem of rebellion against God, the rejection of his laws and the consequence of these actions.

What had gone wrong?

Ezekiel spells this out, with a direct word from God in Ezekiel 5. He is speaking to Jerusalem, the city he has chosen, the place he had established 'in the centre of the nations' (Ezekiel 5:5) and he is accusing the people of turning away from him.

Yet in her wickedness she has rebelled against my laws and decrees more than the nations and countries around her. She has rejected my laws and has not followed my decrees. (Ezekiel 5:6)

Some alarming charges that God brings against his people:

- That they have been wicked, and that this wickedness had led to rebellion against the ways God had told them to live
- That they have even been more disobedient than other nations around them
- That they had rejected God's laws and not followed his decrees

While these charges sound serious, there is nothing explicit about God's name and how this behaviour impacted its honour. So, it is important to recognise how God saw the people of Israel, how he expected them to live in relationship with him, and how that was seen by the nations around them.

One of the things that comes through clearly in the Old Testament is that the people of Israel had a special standing in God's sight, that he had chosen them, that they were "His" in a way that was not true for the other nations. This is spelled out in a number of places, such as Deuteronomy 32:8-9 (which admittedly has caused some confusion!)

When the Most High gave the nations their inheritance, when he divided all mankind, he set up boundaries for the peoples according to the number of the sons of Israel. For the LORD's portion is his people, Jacob his allotted inheritance. (Deuteronomy 32:8–9).

This passage speaks about a time when God divided up the nations (maybe referring to the events around the tower of Babel described in Genesis 11:1-9). And without getting into the complexities of what is meant by "sons of Israel" when speaking about a time before Israel was born,[23] it is clear that God has chosen to engage specifically with the people of Israel. Behind this, is the idea that God has given spiritual beings some form of oversight of earthly nations, but he has reserved Israel for himself.

Earlier in Deuteronomy, Moses reminds the people of the blessing they have been brought into in the closeness of their relationship with God and the laws he has given them.

See, I have taught you decrees and laws as the LORD my God commanded me, so that you may follow them in the land you are entering to take possession of it. Observe them carefully, for this will show your wisdom and understanding to the nations, who will hear about all these decrees and say, 'Surely this great nation is a wise and understanding people.' What other nation is so great as to have their gods near them the way the LORD our God is near us whenever we pray to him? And what other nation is so great as to have such righteous decrees and laws as this body of laws I am setting before you today? (Deuteronomy 4:5–8)

He points out the privilege of their position and speaks of the impact it will have on the nations around them.

---

[23] For some background to this issue, please see J. A. Thompson, *Deuteronomy: An Introduction and Commentary*, vol. 5, Tyndale Old Testament Commentaries (Downers Grove, IL: InterVarsity Press, 1974), 326.

No other nation had the same intimate relationship with their gods as the people of Israel had with theirs. He had acted on their behalf to bring them out of Egypt (Exodus 12:51), he had appeared to them on Mount Sinai (Exodus 19), his presence had been with them through all of their journeys (Exodus 13:21; 33:14), he had provided food and water for them (Exodus 15:25; 16:11-15; 17:5-7), he had brought them to the border of the land he had promised their ancestors hundreds of years previously (Deuteronomy 2:7,14), he had protected them (Deuteronomy 2:24-3:3). No other nations had similar experience or relationship with their gods, this was a unique and privileged situation to be in.

In addition, there was something special about the laws that God had given them – here described as righteous decrees and laws. As we read through the laws that God gave to his people through Moses, we find a wide variety. Some are focusing on big questions – the relationship with God (Exodus 20:2; Leviticus 19:1-2), the importance of family (Exodus 20:12, 14, 17; 21:15, 17), the sanctity of life (Exodus 20:13; Leviticus 19:16), respect for property (Exodus 20:15) and so forth. Others are looking at details such as how priests are to shave (Leviticus 21:5), how clothing should be made (Leviticus 19:19), what harvesting practices should be in place (Leviticus 19:9-10), how they should respond to mold on houses (Leviticus 14:33-55), etc.

From our perspective, we might see some of these laws as being strange and difficult to understand the reasons for them. Some we might see as unnecessarily restrictive and unfair. But they are presented here as righteous, laws that – if followed – would result in good and harmonious society. And the observance of these laws would be noticed by the nations around them who would recognise their wisdom and merit.

Living according to these laws was one way in which God's promise that they would be a blessing to the nations around them would be fulfilled. But, sadly, this is not how it worked out as God's people had an ever-changing relationship with God's law. There are even hints of this in Deuteronomy as Moses reflects on how, even in these early days, God's people had become corrupt and were no longer living as his children (Deuteronomy 32:5). And this continued throughout their history. The psalmist reflected on God's law and rejoiced in it (Psalm 119:70,72) and Josiah worked hard to obey the law (2 Kings 23:24-25). But others, such as Nadab (1 Kings 15:26), Omri (1 Kings 16:25) and Ahab (1 Kings 16:30) were disobedient to God, did not live according to his laws and led the people astray.

No longer were they a people living according to a higher set of standards based on a deeper relationship with a holy and just God, but they were flouting those laws and not even living up to the standards of the nations around them and Ezekiel makes this point explicitly:

'Therefore this is what the Sovereign LORD says: you have been more unruly than the nations around you and have not followed my decrees or kept my laws. You have not even conformed to the standards of the nations around you. (Ezekiel 5:7)

The bar had been lowered and they were not even clearing that!

This would have sent out a clear signal to the nations around them that the standards they had been set, and the God who had set them, were no longer important to them; they were no longer living that way in relationship with their God. So instead of their actions demonstrating the uniqueness and greatness of God, their actions were saying that he was no more to be recognised than any other god. This was not honouring God's name, this was bringing God's name into disrepute.

What was God going to do about it?

God's promised response was frightening – or it would have been if the people had still been concerned about what God thought about them. This response is summarised in Ezekiel 5:8 with much of the rest of the chapter spelling out what it would mean in detail.

"*Therefore this is what the Sovereign* LORD *says: I myself am against you, Jerusalem, and I will inflict punishment on you in the sight of the nations.*" (Ezekiel 5:8)

The NLT makes this even more explicit:

Therefore, I myself, the Sovereign LORD, *am now your enemy. I will punish you publicly while all the nations watch.* (Ezekiel 5:8)

The first thing God speaks about is his change in attitude towards the people; the second is what he is going to do consequently.

Instead of being "for them", God is now setting himself up in opposition against them, instead of watching out for them he is going to see them as his enemy. A painful thing for God to do, the God who loved these people so deeply. A terrifying moment for the people as their protection and security was removed.

We can imagine parallel situations:

- a loving parent, rejected by his children and their attitudes towards him, coming to the painful conclusion that their relationship was broken and he was now opposed to them
- political colleagues falling out resulting in bitterness and challenge replacing friendship and cooperation
- a husband and wife, following their sad breakdown of their marriage due to unfaithfulness, acting against each other as they go through divorce proceedings

Things that were once solid and dependable are now broken, the things that provided stability and security have been removed.

But God does not stop at declaring himself as their enemy, he goes on to say he is going to act against them. Where, previously, God had worked to protect and provide for his people, now he is going to punish them. And this is not to be done in private but exposed to the gaze of the nations around. 'Since the people of God refused to be an example of righteousness and godliness, they would be an example of chastening'.[24] One of the things God is making clear to his people, and to the nations around, is that he will defend the honour of his name even if that means punishing his chosen people.

---

[24] Lamar Eugene Cooper, *Ezekiel*, vol. 17, The New American Commentary (Nashville: Broadman & Holman Publishers, 1994), 103.

The list of things God will do is shocking: because of his actions parents and children will eat each other (indicating a siege with a desperate shortage of food) – something God had predicted through Moses hundreds of years earlier (Leviticus 26:29); he would scatter them; many of them would die due to plague, famine, war and the attacks of wild animals.

There is no mention here of the opportunity for repentance, returning to God and asking him to stop. There is nothing the people can do to prevent God acting against them, they just need to accept it. Until God has done what he sets out to do, until his anger is spent, until he has been avenged for all the ways his people have acted against him. And when that time comes, they will know that this is something God has done to them as he acted to defend the honour of his name (Ezekiel 5:13).

The nations around will see this, they will mock the people of Israel, but they will also recognise the danger of going against God (Ezekiel 5:15). With the people of Israel flouting God's laws for so long there would have been the danger of the surrounding nations concluding that God was unable to do anything about it. But his actions here would have totally dispelled that idea, it would have been clear that God was fully able to defend his name even if his own people were not prepared to do so.

In grace, God had allowed the people to continue in their wickedness for a long time. He had repeatedly called on them to repent, to turn back to him but they had chosen not to. Here God shows that he will not let rebellion continue forever: he will act, his power will be demonstrated; his name will be restored.

There is nothing in this chapter about recovery and restoration for the people - that will come later. The focus here is on God acting in judgment against his rebellious people so that the nations around will see and so that his people will recognise that He has done so.

Leaders getting it wrong

One of the really troubling things we see in Ezekiel is how some of those in positions of authority, those who have been appointed by God to keep his people faithful to him, are – instead – acting against God's laws and leading others astray.

We saw an example of this earlier and we will look at this more generally in this chapter by looking at some occurrences of this in Ezekiel 22. And we will see that this raises important questions for those in positions of authority over God's people today. It will also be important to think about how those under authority should respond to and engage with their leaders.

The 'princes of Israel'

The first group who are challenged for their behaviour are the "princes of Israel", those who are ruling the people and in positions of political power. It is not just an isolated incident as each of them are using their 'power to shed blood' (Ezekiel 6:22). A shocking indictment on those who should be providing for, protecting, caring for the people. This charge of "shedding blood" recurs in this section (vv6, 9, 12) and goes against the command to not murder (Exodus 20:13) and ignores the earlier word of God to Noah about the sanctity of human life (Genesis 9:5-6).

This opening statement is followed by a list (in verses 7-12) of the specific crimes these rules are being charged with – with each one of them going directly against the commands God had given to his people and by the laws that these rulers should be administering.

1. In verse 7 we see:
    a. They were treating parents with contempt in direct disobedience to the fifth commandment where the people of God are called to honour their parents (Exodus 20:12; Deuteronomy 5:16) with an explicit curse being threatened against those who fail to do so (Deuteronomy 27:16)

  b. They have oppressed foreigners, the fatherless and the widow – three groups of people who were to be treated with honour and respect (Exodus 22:21-22; Deuteronomy 24:17) and where, again, going against this was to result in a curse (Deuteronomy 27:19)
2. Verse 8 turns its focus to how these rulers have treated the things of God:
  a. They have despised things that were holy, set apart for God. This was in direct disobedience to the many instances of the Pentateuch where the people were commanded to respect the sacred status of the objects dedicated to the worship of God: the offerings (Exodus 29:33-34); the altar (Exodus 29:37); the special anointing oil (Exodus 30:32) and so forth. There was even recognition that the people might sin unintentionally against these holy things and a specific offering was commanded to make restitution (Leviticus 5:14-16). But the rulers here are being accused of intentionally not honouring these things that God had called sacred
  b. They have desecrated (or violated or profaned) the sabbath, days that were to be set apart for God. This is in direct violation of the third commandment – a commandment that was given to recognise the powerful work of God in creation (Exodus 20:8-11) and how he had rescued his people from slavery in Egypt (Deuteronomy 5:12-15)
3. Verse 9 has a further list of crimes these rulers were committing:
  a. They were engaging in slander (which could mean they were gossiping about others) which was expressly forbidden (Exodus 23:1; Leviticus 19:16). The people were commanded to speak truthfully regarding their neighbours (Exodus 20:16) and this was clearly being broken
  b. And added to their slander was once again the intent to shed blood, to wound, to kill (see earlier comment)

       c. They were also acting immorally – with this idea being expanded on in the next two verses where the focus is on inappropriate sexual behaviour
4. Verses 10 and 11 go into more specifics about these immoral acts – each of which went against what God had called for in his people:
       a. They were 'dishonouring their father's bed' (i.e., having sexual relations with their mother or stepmother) in direct violation of Leviticus 18:7-8, an act that was punishable by death (Leviticus 20:11)
       b. They were having sexual relations with a woman during her period in direct violation of Leviticus 18:19, an act that was punishable by being expelled from the community (Leviticus 20:18)
       c. They were having sexual relations with their neighbour's wife – having been commanded against both adultery (the act) in Exodus 20:14 and coveting (the desire) in Exodus 20:17
       d. They were sexually defiling their daughters-in-law – another act that was punishable by death (Leviticus 20:12)
       e. They were even violating their sisters – again something that was expressly forbidden (Leviticus 18:9)
5. Verse 12 brings this sorry list to an end with statements about more crimes:
       a. Accepting any sort of bribe was expressly forbidden as it could diminish the impartiality of justice (Exodus 23:8; Deuteronomy 16:19). But taking a bribe to shed blood was even worse and expressly stated as something that would result in being cursed (Deuteronomy 27:25)
       b. Taking interest and making profit from the poor was expressly forbidden (Exodus 22:25) and, in fact, charging interest to any fellow Israelite was against the law (Deuteronomy 22:19)

       c. It concludes with the statement that they had forgotten God:
          i. They no longer had any thought for God
          ii. They no longer cared for his commandments
          iii. They no longer cared for the people he had placed in their charge

The text does not suggest that all these rulers were doing all these things but that each of these things were being carried out by at least some of the rulers – and there was no attempt by the others to stop them.

This list is added to, or summarised, in verse 25 where we see that the princes were conspiring together in order to take what they wanted, to destroy, to kill.

A shocking condemnation of how far these people had come from the role God had intended for them – to be models and examples of how God's people should live and to enforce God's laws when they saw them being broken.

And is it any wonder that God is going to respond to washing his hands of them, to deal with them, to scatter them among the nations, to put an end to their wrongdoing. With the expectation that when he does this, and not until them, will they recognise again that God is still God, that he is still in total authority and power (Ezekiel 22:13-16).

But how had it come to this? Why were these princes living in such a way, totally opposed to the lives they were called to lead and the responsibilities they were to discharge? They had been placed in a position of privilege that brought with it obligations – but they were exploiting this and tearing down instead of building up; setting a really bad example instead of showing the people how to live as the children of God.

It would probably started with the statement at the end of verse 12:

And you have forgotten me, declares the Sovereign LORD. (Ezekiel 22:12b)

This is not saying that these princes no longer knew about God but that they had deliberately chosen to ignore, to disobey, the covenant agreement he had set in place with them.[25] This would have led on to them ceasing to love God as their first duty (Deuteronomy 6:5) and then ceasing to love their neighbour (Leviticus 19:18) as they should. These were the central guiding commands of the covenant, required for all God's people, to be modelled by the leaders of those people, and turning away from them would have been quickly followed by the list of offences outlined in Ezekiel 22:6-11.

It is as though they had become too convinced of their own importance and come to believe that the rules no longer applied to them. Instead of living to bless, guide and provide for others they were living purely for themselves out for whatever they could get, for whatever they wanted.

Other groups in authority

Sadly, the charges do not stop with the 'princes of Israel' but other groups are also not living up to the expectations on them. Before getting into the detail, it is worth noting there is some uncertainty over what is meant by how these groups of people are described.

Comparing the NIV and ESV translations, for example, we have:

Verse	NIV	ESV
25	princes	prophets
26	priests	priests
27	officials	princes
28	prophets	prophets

---

[25] Daniel Isaac Block, *The Book of Ezekiel, Chapters 1–24*, The New International Commentary on the Old Testament (Grand Rapids, MI: Wm. B. Eerdmans Publishing Co., 1997), 711.

These differences are, mainly, dependent on whether the translators based their work on the Hebrew or Greek texts of the Old Testament. Whichever translation is adopted, it is clear that different groups of people, people in positions of authority, were exploiting their positions and doing harm to the people. In the discussion that follows, the NIV reading is assumed.

The priests

The first group spoken about, in addition to the princes, was the priests:

Her priests do violence to my law and profane my holy things; they do not distinguish between the holy and the common; they teach that there is no difference between the unclean and the clean; and they shut their eyes to the keeping of my Sabbaths, so that I am profaned among them. (Ezekiel 22:26)

Again, the charges are shocking.

Priests were in place to do some key things within the context of religious practice:

1. To act as religious leaders
2. To perform religious rites on behalf of someone else: a worshipper; someone was seeking forgiveness
3. To act as mediators between the people and God

These were important and vital roles in helping the people stay close to God and within their covenant relationship. But, as the charges here make clear, they were not doing any of these things – rather they were doing the opposite.

One of the clearly stated, persistent, responsibilities of the priest was to be able to distinguish between the 'holy and common' and the 'unclean and clean' so that they could teach the people how to obey God's law (Leviticus 10:10-11). But they were ignoring that responsibility and teaching the people that touching anything, eating anything, living in any way they liked, was acceptable. Similarly, they were turning a blind eye to non-observance of the Sabbath – ignoring that keeping it was one of the key requirements of the law.

With the religious leaders ignoring the law and saying religious observance did not matter, it is no wonder that God charges them with profaning, or dishonouring, his name.

The officials

The list does not stop there. The next group of people who are singled out are the 'officials.

Her officials within her are like wolves tearing their prey; they shed blood and kill people to make unjust gain. (Ezekiel 22:27)

These people operate at a lower level than the princes, they were people who kept the state running, who administered its laws and so forth. Some equivalent positions today would include judges, civil servants, council leaders, the police, etc. People relied on to keep things operating as they should be, to act for the good of the wider community. But, instead, they were following the example of the princes, ignoring their responsibilities, and taking what they could get. As a consequence, they are a burden to the people, directly causing them harm, as opposed to being a blessing to them.

Seeing the behaviour of their superiors it is maybe not surprising that they conformed to that way of living, but they were each responsible for their own actions and those actions were not pleasing to God.

The prophets

And then there were the prophets. People called by God to speak God's word to the people with one of their specific responsibilities being to challenge those in authority when they were being disobedient to God's law or failing to rule in line with God's will.

There are many examples of prophets doing this, such as:

- Nathan rebuking David for his sin with Bathsheba (2 Samuel 12:1-14)
- Elijah challenging Ahab (1 Kings 18:18)

- Micaiah speaking out against Ahab and Jehoshaphat (1 Kings 22:17-28)
- Isaiah warning of judgment because of what was happening in his day (Isaiah 9:8-10:4)

This is how the prophets were supposed to respond when they saw God's people, particularly those in positions of authority, rebelling against him. An opportunity for people to hear God's word, to recognise their wrongdoing, to turn back in obedience to God.

But this is not how the prophets were responding in the time of Ezekiel:

Her prophets whitewash these deeds for them by false visions and lying divinations. They say, 'This is what the Sovereign LORD says'—when the LORD has not spoken. (Ezekiel 22:28)

Rather they were seeing everything that was going on and providing "cover" for them – they were endorsing their wicked deeds, claiming it was in accordance with what God had told them, when it clearly was not.

The 'people of the land'

And the last group were just the ordinary people in the land. They were not people in positions of authority or power but, having seen how those who were in those positions were behaving, seemed to have taken the attitude "if it's all right for them, it's all right for us". And so they were joining in with these wicked practices and exploiting their neighbours in many different ways.

The people of the land practice extortion and commit robbery; they oppress the poor and needy and mistreat the foreigner, denying them justice. (Ezekiel 22:29)

A reminder to those in authority that their actions and example can have significant consequence for those over whom they have been placed.

The focus on defending the honour of God's name

In the preceding three chapters, we have looked at some of what was going on among God's people. We have seen that idolatry, worshipping and serving false gods, was prevalent across all levels of society; we have thought about those who were disobeying God's law; we have recognised that some of those in authority were leading others astray. In all of these areas the first two commandments (Exodus 20:3-6) are being smashed and God's name is not being honoured in direct violation of the third commandment:

'You shall not misuse the name of the LORD your God, for the LORD will not hold anyone guiltless who misuses his name. (Exodus 20:7)

This only matters if God cares that his name is being brought into disrepute, if observing the third commandment is still important to him. If it is of no consequence to him then this state of affairs could continue indefinitely. This chapter will argue that God's name is still very important to him and something to be defended as a matter of high priority. This means that he and his people are travelling very different paths, and something needs to change.

Having established this fact, the next two chapters will look at some of the attributes and actions of God to gain a better understanding of who he is, what is important to him and why he does what he does often to defend that name.

In this chapter, we are going to look at four passages in Ezekiel where God speaks directly about his name and refers to the actions he has taken, and will take, to defend it.

Ezekiel 20 – Exodus and Exile

In Ezekiel 20:9, God explains why he had rescued his people from slavery in Egypt:

But for the sake of my name, I brought them out of Egypt. I did it to keep my name from being profaned in the eyes of the nations among whom they lived and in whose sight I had revealed myself to the Israelites. (Ezekiel 20:9)

There are various reasons given in the Bible for why God brought his people out of Egypt:

- In Genesis 15:14, God promises to Abram that he will bring his descendants out of slavery
- In Exodus 3:7-10 God tells Moses that he is 'concerned about their suffering' and that he has seen how they are being oppressed and so he is going to send Moses to bring them out of Egypt.
- Hosea suggests that God does this because he loved them, as a father loves a son (Hosea 11:1)

So a range of reasons are given: love, concern, fulfilling a promise. And they all contribute something to our understanding of why God acted as he did in rescuing his people. But here, in Ezekiel, we are given another perspective – that God did this for the sake of his name.

As we saw earlier, when thinking about the long-term problem of idolatry, God was going to punish his people, even while still in Egypt, for the way in which they had turned against him (Ezekiel 20:8). This would have resulted in the people of Egypt concluding that God was unable to do what he had committed to do and so his reputation would have been damaged. So even though God was angry with the people for their idolatry, acting to protect the honour of his name took priority over punishing them and so he brought them out.

How would they have responded to that act of grace in the face of disobedience? Would they have realised how sinful they had been and resolved to be more obedient to God or would they have become more confident in wrong-doing, thinking they could get away with it and God would still watch over them? Unfortunately, in general, the latter seems to have been the case as their story unfolds.

A little later on, in the wilderness, God again announced that he would punish them for their ongoing disobedience but, again, spared them because of how it would have been perceived by the nations around them:

But for the sake of my name I did what would keep it from being profaned in the eyes of the nations in whose sight I had brought them out. (Ezekiel 20:14)

This is described in Exodus 32, the incident of the golden calf, where Moses pleads with God to not destroy the people so that the people of Egypt could not say that he had rescued them with evil purposes in mind (Exodus 32:12).

Ezekiel 20:18-20 goes on to explain that, during the wilderness journey, God spoke to the children of the rescued community, encouraging them to not follow in the sinful steps of their parents but to stay faithful to God. But the children followed the practices of their parents resulting in God planning to pour out his anger against this second generation (Ezekiel 20:21-22).

But, again, God held back from punishing them so that his name was not dishonoured in the view of the nations around, but God also said that, because of their disobedience, he would send them away into exile into foreign lands.

But I withheld my hand, and for the sake of my name I did what would keep it from being profaned in the eyes of the nations in whose sight I had brought them out. Also with uplifted hand I swore to them in the wilderness that I would disperse them among the nations and scatter them through the countries, because they had not obeyed my laws but had rejected my decrees and desecrated my Sabbaths, and their eyes lusted after their parents' idols. (Ezekiel 20:22–24)

God is acting to defend the honour of his name:

- firstly, by choosing not to destroy the people of Israel as that would give the surrounding nations opportunity to accuse him of not being able to follow through on his promises
- secondly, by preparing to punish disobedience by sending the people of Israel into exile

His strength and power had been amply demonstrated to his people and the surrounding nations through many ways as he had rescued them, brought them through the wilderness, driven out enemies before them, established them in the land he had promised, performed many miraculous acts amongst them. In doing so, he defended the honour of his name even as his own people rebelled against him. And then, with that honour clearly established, he acted in accordance with his promises to continue to defend his name by sending his rebellious people away into exile.

But even in exile God was going to continue to be their God and, eventually, he would rescue them again, bring them back into the land into accordance with his promises. This act of powerful restoration would result in God being demonstrated to be holy among the nations and his people, once again, recognising that he is their Lord:

I will accept you as fragrant incense when I bring you out from the nations and gather you from the countries where you have been scattered, and I will be proved holy through you in the sight of the nations. Then you will know that I am the LORD, when I bring you into the land of Israel, the land I had sworn with uplifted hand to give to your ancestors. (Ezekiel 20:41–42)

They will recognise the error of their sinful ways, they will turn back to God as he deals with them in accordance with preserving the honour of his name:

You will know that I am the LORD, when I deal with you for my name's sake and not according to your evil ways and your corrupt practices, you people of Israel, declares the Sovereign LORD." ' (Ezekiel 20:44)

From Egypt through wilderness through promised land through exile and to future restoration God chooses to act to defend the honour of his name so that this is recognised by his chosen people.

Ezekiel 36 – Hope and Holiness

But it is not enough that God's people recognise the honour of his name, God will act to ensure that the surrounding nations do as well.

One of the interesting things about Ezekiel 36 is that it starts with a message of hope from God – but a message that is directed towards the land rather than directly to his people. He speaks out against the nations who have ravaged the land (Ezekiel 36:4) and pledges that he will heap scorn and suffering upon them in turn (Ezekiel 36:7). He goes on to make some powerful promises about how the land is going to be restored:

- That it will provide what is needed for the exiles who will soon be returning (Ezekiel 36:8)
- That it will soon be cultivated with towns being rebuilt and inhabited as the people return (Ezekiel 36:9-10)
- That more people and animals will live there again (Ezekiel 36:11)
- That God's people will live in the land again and never leave (Ezekiel 36:12)

A message of hope for the land, carrying a corresponding message of hope for the people who will return to inhabit that land and make it prosperous once again. This hope is spelled out later in the chapter as God turns his focus towards his people – first reminding them of why they were in exile and then promising to bring them home.

In verses 17-21, God speaks about their wickedness and idolatry and how he had acted to send them into exile. But he recognises that wherever they went in exile his name had been brought into disrepute:

And wherever they went among the nations they profaned my holy name, for it was said of them, "These are the LORD's people, and yet they had to leave his land." (Ezekiel 36:20)

The nations are effectively concluding that God was unable to keep his people safe which resulted in them being defeated and taken away into exile. And this caused God to be concerned:

I had concern for my holy name, which the people of Israel profaned among the nations where they had gone. (Ezekiel 36:21)

God sent the people into exile to be faithful to his promises, but he was not prepared for the nations to which he had sent them to think inappropriately about him as a result. So he decided to act and to bring his people home.

But just as we saw earlier that God's reason for bringing the people out of Egypt was to defend the honour of his name, so here we see that this is the reason for bringing them back out of exile:

'Therefore say to the Israelites, "This is what the Sovereign LORD says: it is not for your sake, people of Israel, that I am going to do these things, but for the sake of my holy name, which you have profaned among the nations where you have gone. I will show the holiness of my great name, which has been profaned among the nations, the name you have profaned among them. Then the nations will know that I am the LORD, declares the Sovereign LORD, when I am proved holy through you before their eyes. (Ezekiel 36:22–23)

The rest of the chapter goes on to speak about the many blessings the people will experience as they come back into the land but, even in that, God again makes it clear he is not doing it for them or because they deserved it:

I want you to know that I am not doing this for your sake, declares the Sovereign LORD. Be ashamed and disgraced for your conduct, people of Israel! (Ezekiel 36:32)

God is saying to his people that he will defend the honour of his name by what he does for them even though they do not deserve it. This gives an insight into how important God's name, and how he is perceived, is to him.

A defence lawyer is expected to defend someone to the best of his ability even if he believes that person to be guilty – because the principles of justice and the law are more important than how the behaviour of the person he is defending.

A surgeon or doctor will work to save the life of a convicted murderer to uphold the standards of their profession.

Organisations, societies and nations are diminished when these standards are seen to drop, and it can take a lot of work and a lot of time for those standards to be lifted and credibility to be restored.

God was not prepared for his name to continue to be held in disrepute by the nations and so he acted to restore the honour of his name even though his people did not deserve it.

Ezekiel 39 – Victory over the Nations

In Ezekiel 38, the prophet is called to speak out against a ruler called Gog (Ezekiel 38:1) who leads powerful armies from the north (Ezekiel 38:6). As the story develops, we see this prince preparing for war against a land that he sees as defenceless before him. But he fails to recognise that God is directing him so that the surrounding nations will recognise God's holiness:

You will advance against my people Israel like a cloud that covers the land. In days to come, Gog, I will bring you against my land, so that the nations may know me when I am proved holy through you before their eyes. (Ezekiel 38:16)

This will happen by God pouring out judgment on Gog who will be totally defeated resulting in God's greatness being seen and recognised (Ezekiel 38:17-23).

This story raises many questions about how God acts in the world and how he sometimes seems to act against those who are doing what he has called them to do. But for our purposes here, the key thing is what God is doing to defend his name and we see this in chapter 39.

As he acts, he makes clear that the result of this will be his name being recognised and not being brought into disrepute:

' *"I will make known my holy name among my people Israel. I will no longer let my holy name be profaned, and the nations will know that I the LORD am the Holy One in Israel.* (Ezekiel 39:7)

And this is spelled out in more detail later in the chapter. In verses 21-24, God provides his perspective on what is going on and makes it clear that this act of judgment is going to raise his standing. It is going to cause his people to recognise who he is while the nations will recognise that the reason for the exile was the unfaithfulness of God's people and not any inability of God to keep them safe.

And he does this because he is zealous for his name:

'*Therefore this is what the Sovereign LORD says: I will now restore the fortunes of Jacob and will have compassion on all the people of Israel, and I will be zealous for my holy name.* (Ezekiel 39:25)

Ezekiel 43 – Glory Restored

As mentioned earlier, one of the implications of the unfaithfulness and disobedience of God's people was that God's presence and glory had left the Temple (Ezekiel 10). And in Ezekiel 43, we saw that glory returning.

The exile had happened, the people had returned, God was going to demonstrate his supreme power over the nations, and the final act is for his presence to return to the Temple in glory.

And as he does so, there is a statement about the future and reminder of what had happened – and it is all about God's name.

The statement about the future is one of hope, of confidence – that God's people will never again defile his name through their actions:

He said: 'Son of man, this is the place of my throne and the place for the soles of my feet. This is where I will live among the Israelites for ever. The people of Israel will never again defile my holy name—neither they nor their kings—by their prostitution and the funeral offerings for their kings at their death. (Ezekiel 43:7)

God was restating his commitment to the people, was reclaiming Jerusalem to be his city and the Temple to be where his people could meet with him. And he is stating that his people will never again fail in the way they had done, they will never dishonour his name again as they had been doing for so long.

The reminder is of the many ways in which God's people had defiled his name and the actions he had taken in response. This is followed by a call to live as his faithful people once again with the promise that he would continue to live amongst them:

When they placed their threshold next to my threshold and their doorposts beside my doorposts, with only a wall between me and them, they defiled my holy name by their detestable practices. So I destroyed them in my anger. Now let them put away from me their prostitution and the funeral offerings for their kings, and I will live among them for ever. (Ezekiel 43:8–9)

A message of hope, a message of recommitment, a promise of living in unity once again.

The glory of God

Thinking about the glory of God

"Glory" is one of those words used in many different contexts:
- People speak about "glorious weather"
- Cricket commentators will get excited about a "glorious cover drive"
- Tourists will gaze at a "glorious view"
- Military historians will reflect on "glorious victories" that were seen to change the course of history

The term carries the sense of something that is of great intrinsic worth and value, something to be recognised and praised. So it speaks about the nature of something as well as speaking about how people respond to it.

The Merriam-Webster dictionary picks up on these ideas by defining glory by being, on one hand, honour given to something worthy while, on the other hand, being something that has within itself attributes that are worthy of praise.[26]

So, it is hardly surprising that this term is used to describe some of God's attributes: his majesty, his power, his creative acts, his work in salvation. And it is hardly surprising that his people respond by "giving him glory".

The seraphim in Isaiah's vision recognised this as they called to one another:

'Holy, holy, holy is the LORD Almighty; the whole earth is full of his glory.' (Isaiah 6:3b).

---

[26] Inc Merriam-Webster, *Merriam-Webster's Collegiate Dictionary*. (Springfield, MA: Merriam-Webster, Inc., 2003).

The glory of God as seen in Jesus

God's presence is often indicated by signs of his glory, and this is most perfectly demonstrated in Jesus.

John makes this clear at the beginning of his Gospel:

The Word became flesh and made his dwelling among us. We have seen his glory, the glory of the one and only Son, who came from the Father, full of grace and truth. (John 1:14)

The obvious account in the life of Jesus that speaks about him revealing his eternal glory is in the story of the Transfiguration. But this story, while told in each of the Synoptic Gospels (Matthew 17:1-9; Mark 9:2-10; Luke 9:28-36), is absent from John. So John must have something else in mind – some other events that revealed the glory of Jesus, the glory of God, and told in the Gospel.

We see the beginning of this as Jesus turns water into wine in a wedding at Cana, demonstrating some of the great power that was available to him. This is referred to as the 'first of the signs through which he revealed his glory' (John 2:11).

When Jesus hears of the sickness of Lazarus, he tells his followers that this will be an opportunity for God to be glorified – and for him to be glorified through it (John 11:4).

When Greeks requested an audience with Jesus, Jesus recognised this as a sign and responded by saying that it was now the time for 'the Son of Man to be glorified' (John 12:23). As he continues, Jesus makes it clear that this glorification will happen through death, signifying that the place of his ultimate glorification on earth would be on the cross.

This becomes even more immediate as, recognising that Judas had gone to betray him, Jesus tells his remaining followers that at that moment the Son of Man, himself, was glorified (John 13:31).

For John, and for his readers, it was the demonstration of power – over physical things and death itself – and, ultimately, in what Jesus accomplished on the cross that enabled them to see the glory of Jesus.

This recognition of the glory of Jesus is picked up in the opening verses of Hebrews

In the past God spoke to our ancestors through the prophets at many times and in various ways, but in these last days he has spoken to us by his Son, whom he appointed heir of all things, and through whom also he made the universe. The Son is the radiance of God's glory and the exact representation of his being, sustaining all things by his powerful word. After he had provided purification for sins, he sat down at the right hand of the Majesty in heaven. (Hebrews 1:1–3)

The word translated 'radiance' here does not appear anywhere else in the New Testament and can either refer to the radiation of light from a source, such as our sun, or the reflection of that light, such as from the moon.[27] While there are commentators who favour both views, Craig Koester's comment is helpful as he points out that this is talking about how 'God communicates *through* the Son', that the Son is the one who brings the reality of God's glory into the world we live in.[28] It is in and through Jesus that we see the glory of God revealed.

This is recognised, again, as all of creation unites together in God's throne room to speak out words of praise to God and to the Lamb who had been slain and recognise that they are worthy of 'praise and honour and glory and power' (Revelation 5:13).

The glory of God in the Old Testament

God's glory is spoken of in many ways in the Old Testament:

- Demonstrated in creation (Psalm 19:1-2)
- Greater than all of creation (Psalm 113:4)
- Seen through the events of the Exodus (Exodus 14:4, 17)
- Something that Moses desired to experience in a deeper way (Exodus 33:18-23, 34:5-7)
- Revealed to his chosen people (Leviticus 9:23) and through them to the surrounding nations (Isaiah 44:23)

---

[27] Peter T. O'Brien, *The Letter to the Hebrews*, The Pillar New Testament Commentary (Grand Rapids, MI; Nottingham, England: William B. Eerdmans Publishing Company, 2010), 54.
[28] Craig R. Koester, *Hebrews: A New Translation with Introduction and Commentary*, vol. 36, Anchor Yale Bible (New Haven; London: Yale University Press, 2008), 180.

But one of the repeated places we see it occurring is in the places God chose to come and meet with his people, to demonstrate the reality of his presence among them.

When all the components for the tabernacle were ready and Moses took the final steps of fitting all the pieces together (Exodus 40:17-33), God's glory came down and filled it (Exodus 40:34). It was a permanent sign of God's presence and while the cloud, representing that presence, stayed in the tabernacle the people of Israel stayed where they were (Exodus 40:36-38).

When the temple in Jerusalem was completed and the are brought into it, the cloud of God's presence, the glory of God, filled it (1 Kings 8:10-11).

The Temple was to be a permanent sign of God's presence among his people in the place that he had chosen to establish his name (2 Kings 21:7). But, as the people of God and their rulers, continue to rebel against Him, God warns that this is going to change – that the people living in Jerusalem would be sent away, that Jerusalem and the temple would be rejected (2 Kings 23:26-27) and it is this reality we see being described in Ezekiel but, beyond that, there is a message of hope.

The glory of God in Ezekiel

The book of Ezekiel frequently refers to God's glory and it is one of the things that God is defending when he acts to uphold the honour of his name. In this section, we will look at how it is referenced and its implications.

The first time we see God's glory referred to in Ezekiel is at the end of chapter 1. It is a chapter that positions the events that Ezekiel experienced in both time and space – he was 30 years old, in exile by the Kebar River (Ezekiel 1:1). Ezekiel sees an amazing vision: a windstorm, flashing lighting, a fire with four living creatures in the middle of it, sparking wheels full of eyes, topped with an awesome crystalline platform (Ezekiel 1:2-24). Above this platform was a throne, and above the throne was 'a figure like that of a man'. He appeared to be full of fire from the waist up, glowing like molten metal and was surrounded by brilliant light like a rainbow (Ezekiel 1:25-28). This is how Ezekiel described what he saw and he recognised that this figure was showing him the glory of the Lord. And his response was to fall facedown on the ground – maybe in fear, maybe in worship, maybe as a recognition that this was all outside of his understanding and experience. Even in exile, far away from the land of his birth and the Temple of his God, Ezekiel was able to experience something of God's glory and to recognise his greatness. It would have gained his attention, it resulted in him falling on the ground. It is as though God's glory was the first thing God wanted Ezekiel to recognise, something that would remind him of God's greatness, something that would prepare him for the call God was going to make on his life.

From this place of encounter, God calls Ezekiel to go to his people in exile and to speak God's word to them. And as Ezekiel received his commission, he heard a loud sound as the 'glory of the Lord rose from the place where it was standing' (Ezekiel 3:12). God's hand was on him, God's spirit was guiding him, but the glory of God did not go with him as he was sent to the people who had rebelled against God and were in exile as a consequence. We are left wondering whether God's glory will return to his people or not.

Seven days later, God speaks again to Ezekiel and explains that his role is going to be that of a watchman – someone to whom God will speak and who will then pass on God's word to the people. God makes it clear that Ezekiel's responsibility ends at passing on God's message – the people themselves are responsible for how they respond (Ezekiel 3:16-21). And having given Ezekiel this task, God calls him to go out to a nearby plain where he once again experienced the glory of the Lord resulting in him, again, falling facedown on the ground (Ezekiel 3:22-23). A reminder of the God who had called him, a reminder of the majesty of his presence, something that would be helpful to Ezekiel as he faced difficulty and resistance from the people to whom God was sending him.

So at his first encounter with God and, again, when God gave him his overall commission, Ezekiel experienced something of God's glory which had a profound impact on him.

The next time we see God's glory mentioned is when it is presented in contrast to the idolatry that God's people still in Jerusalem were engaged in. In Ezekiel 8, Ezekiel is transported in a vision to Jerusalem when he sees the temple with many indications of idolatry (and we examined this earlier). But as Ezekiel was shown idols (Ezekiel 8:5), seventy elders worshipping idols in secret (Ezekiel 8:9-13), women mourning false gods (Ezekiel 8:14), men worshipping the sun (Ezekiel 8:16) he also saw the glory of God again, just as he had previously seen it on the plain (Ezekiel 8:4). Even in the midst of all this idolatry, wickedness and sin God's glory still shone through. The people were not going to respond to it, probably did not even see it, but it was there in Ezekiel's vision. A reminder that God was still majestic, he was still in control, and he was aware of everything that was going on. And that vision would have kept Ezekiel focused on God and the mission he had been given.

But it was not enough to prevent justice falling on those who were committing idolatry and in the next three chapters we are presented with the awful picture of God's glory leaving the Temple as God chose, for a time, to distance himself from his people who had turned against him, who had rebelled for so long. We get a hint of this in Ezekiel 9 as God pronounces judgment on those in Jerusalem and his glory moves to the 'threshold of the temple' (Ezekiel 9:3) as the temple is defiled and people are killed in judgment. But this is completed in Ezekiel 10-11 in a strange and poignant way. At first there is a glimmer of hope as God's glory moves to the threshold of the temple (as though actually putting into effect what had been mentioned in chapter 9) and filling the temple court with its radiance (Ezekiel 9:4). It would have been easy to hope that with that judgment carried out, that God had chosen to demonstrate his glory once again and continue to reside in the Temple and receive the worship of his people. But it was too late for that and, after a brief time that reminded Ezekiel of what had been, God's glory departed through the East gate of the Temple (Ezekiel 10:19) and then out through the city and to the mountains to the East (Ezekiel 11:23). Even in this terrible moment, there is a clear message of hope that the people will return and God would be restored to his place at the centre of his rescued people (Ezekiel 11:16-21) but, for now, God had removed his glory from the place he had chosen but had been defiled by his rebellious people.

Interestingly, the next time we see God's glory mentioned is in Ezekiel 28 in the context of another nation Sidon, when God says that he will display his glory there (Ezekiel 28:22). Sidon was a coastal town on the edge of the Mediterranean and it seems as though, from verse 24, that it, along with many other neighbouring towns, had spoken out against the people of God and rejoiced in their downfall. And, as in the time of Ezekiel, the reputation of a nation's god was tied up in the state of the nation,[29] there was the very high probability that the people of Sidon had seen the defeat of the people of Israel as a sign of the defeat of Israel's God. To address this, God chose to act and to display his glory to the people of Sidon. He was above his people, anything bad that had happened to them did not mean that God's power had failed, nor his glory been diminished, and God was going to demonstrate this powerfully to them. The return of the people of Israel was still in the future but God was still God and was going to demonstrate this by acting in judgment against the nations around. They were to be left in no doubt that, irrespective of what had happened to his people, he was still the Lord (Ezekiel 28:23).

The next reference is in Ezekiel 39, again where God is speaking about judgment on Gog, a prince of a land called Magog.[30] God speaks of a powerful victory against these people and, in doing so, he will be displaying his glory (Ezekiel 39:13). And God lays out the reasons for doing this – reasons that relate to his people, and reasons that relate to the surrounding nations. Firstly, as God displays his glory (Ezekiel 39:21), his people will once again recognise who he is, and who he is in relation to them – he is the 'Lord their God' (Ezekiel 39:21-22). Secondly, the nations will clearly understand that the people of Israel were punished for their unfaithfulness to God and that it was God who had handed them over into exile (Ezekiel 39:23-24). It wasn't that God was unable to keep them safe, but that – in judgment – he acted against his own people. His glory was undimmed, even when it appeared to the nations around that he had been unable to protect his people.

---

[29] Daniel Isaac Block, *The Book of Ezekiel, Chapters 25–48*, The New International Commentary on the Old Testament (Grand Rapids, MI: Wm. B. Eerdmans Publishing Co., 1997–), 125.

[30] These were introduced in Ezekiel 38:1-2.

But this time of judgment is nearly over, God is going to restore his people, to have compassion on them, to bring them home (Ezekiel 39:25-29). From this point in the book the message is all positive as, in stages, God acts to bring the exile to an end. In Ezekiel 40-41, Ezekiel is given a vision of the temple being restored; in Ezekiel 42, provision is made for the priests with the implication that worship is going to be restored. And then, with this preparation out of the way, in Ezekiel 43-44, Ezekiel sees the glory of God returning, as God takes up residence in the temple again. When God's glory had left the temple, it went out to the east of the city (Ezekiel 11:23) and now it returns from the same direction.

and I saw the glory of the God of Israel coming from the east. His voice was like the roar of rushing waters, and the land was radiant with his glory. The vision I saw was like the vision I had seen when he came to destroy the city and like the visions I had seen by the Kebar River, and I fell facedown. The glory of the LORD *entered the temple through the gate facing east. Then the Spirit lifted me up and brought me into the inner court, and the glory of the* LORD *filled the temple.* (Ezekiel 43:2-5)

As we read these words, we get a sense of power and majesty and grandeur is God's glory rushes in from the east, spreading radiance over the entire land. It must have been even more powerful and impressive for Ezekiel as he witnessed God's return. And there is a wonderful progression with God's glory travelling over the land, entering into the temple, filling the temple. And as God's glory returns, so God speaks about this being the place where he will dwell among his people forever (Ezekiel 43:6-9) with the exile behind them and a wonderful future ahead.

And as Ezekiel sees the glory of the Lord filling the temple, he falls and lies facedown on the floor (Ezekiel 44:4), recognising God's presence and holiness and power.

So, throughout this book, we see God's glory appearing to Ezekiel as God commissioned him; God's glory present undimmed even as his people practiced idolatry; God's glory leaving the temple as a sign that God had, for a time, turned against his people; God showing his glory to the surrounding nations as a powerful statement that he was still in control; God's glory returning as he prepared to bring his people home.

God is "the Lord"

Previous chapters in this book have looked at some of the ways in which the relationship between God and his people had broken down. For centuries they had persisted in going after and worshipping other gods, they had disobeyed God in multiple ways, those in authority were leading the people astray. As a consequence, many had been sent away into exile and those who were left in Jerusalem were not in a good place in terms of their relationship with God. And this could lead an observer to assume that, just as the people had turned away from God, so God had turned away from his people and that the relationship that had seemed so important had come to an end.

But one of the clear messages that threads through this book is that God sees things totally differently, that he is still their God, that this will not change and that he is going to act so that everyone knows this to be true. There are 59 times in the book where God says that he is going to do something so that people will know that he is "the Lord" or "the sovereign Lord".[31] In all of these occurrences, the Hebrew word used for Lord is יהוה, or YHWH, the personal name of God.

Many titles are used for God in the Bible, but this one is the name he chooses to identify himself with his people – and it occurs time and time again:

- We come across it for the first time in Genesis 2:4 which speaks of God creating the earth and the heavens where he will dwell with the people he made in his image
- It is the name used when God calls Abram to leave his country and promises to give him the land he will walk across (Genesis 12:1-7)
- God revealed himself to Isaac as this same God (Genesis 26:24) and subsequently did the same for Jacob (Genesis 28:13)
- He was with Joseph and enabled him to prosper even as a slave in Egypt (Genesis 39:2)

---

[31] The first of these is in Ezekiel 6:7 and the last one is in Ezekiel 39:28.

- It was the name God used to refer to himself when telling Moses to go and speak to the people of Israel about the hope of rescue (Exodus 3:15-16) and the name they were to use when going to speak to Pharoah about being allowed to go into the wilderness to worship their God (Exodus 3:18)
- He acted in power against the Egyptian army (Exodus 14:27) causing the people of God to recognise that their God was exalted, a powerful warrior, unique among the gods and a powerful king (Exodus 15:1-18)

There are many more examples, but these demonstrate something of the relationship God had with his chosen people and how he acted on their behalf with great power to bring rich blessing.

As we look through the book of Ezekiel, we find that nothing has changed and that, in spite of how the people had behaved, God was still their God and was going to demonstrate it so that it was totally clear to everyone. But in the majority of cases, this would be devastating for his people as he acted in judgment against them for the years, even centuries, where they had consistently turned against him. As we examine these events spoken about in the book of Ezekiel it can easily raise questions as to how God could do this against his own people, how can this demonstrate that he is in relationship with them, has he eventually given up on them? But are these the questions we should be asking, or is God wanting to challenge us in different ways?

God acting against his people so that they will know him for who he is

Time after time[32] God speaks about what he is going to do against his people so that they will 'know that I am the Lord'. And this action includes killing some of them, bringing destruction on the land, judging the people in a variety of ways, sending even more of them into exile. And there are special warnings for the civic and religious leaders who are setting poor examples and leading God's people away. Shocking and difficult to read and reflect on – but important in deepening our understanding of the lengths God will go to in order to remind his people of his deep commitment to them, and his desire for relationship with them – but also a reminder that this desire needs to be reciprocated or judgment will, eventually, follow.

The first time we see this is in Ezekiel 6:7-14. Here God is calling on Ezekiel to prophesy against the mountains of Israel (Ezekiel 6:1). These mountains represent the whole land of Israel but were also the places where idol worship took place[33] (yet another instance of the problem of chronic, ongoing, idolatry that we discussed earlier). And it seems as though the end of the road has been reached for these places of worship and those who worship there – with the altars being demolished and the idol worshippers being killed (Ezekiel 6:4-5). Throughout history, God had sent judges and prophets to challenge people about the worship of idols and to draw them back into relationship with their God but, while this may have had an impact in the short term, the people reverted to worshipping idols and turning against their God. Various kings – such as Hezekiah (2 Kings 18:1-4) and Josiah (2 Kings 23:1-15) - had tried to stamp out this practice of idol worship but, apart from these attempts, the practice continued (2 Kings 12:3; 15:35; 22:43).

---

[32] Starting in Ezekiel 6 and going through to Ezekiel 33.
[33] Lamar Eugene Cooper, *Ezekiel*, vol. 17, The New American Commentary (Nashville: Broadman & Holman Publishers, 1994), 107

This went totally against what God wanted from, and had demanded of, his people. In Deuteronomy 7:1-10, Moses is preparing the people for entering into the land that God had promised them. He commands them to break their altars and to burn their idols (Deuteronomy 7:5) because of who they were, people chosen by God to be holy and his 'treasured possession' (Deuteronomy 7:6). But even as they receive these commands and are reminded of their unique relationship with God, there is a word of challenge:

But those who hate him he will repay to their face by destruction; he will not be slow to repay to their face those who hate him. (Deuteronomy 7:10)

The warning is clear that those who turn against God, those who put idols in the place that belongs only to God, should expect destruction to follow. And this idea is developed and expanded in Deuteronomy 28:15-68, where warning after warning is given of the consequences of not being fully obedient to God, with these warnings including destruction and ruin (Deuteronomy 28:20-24). The language is graphic and powerful, leaving the people in no doubt of the eventual consequences of disobedience. And this had been experienced to different levels and at different times in the disobedient history of God's people and here, in Ezekiel, God warns that he is going to do it again.

On many occasions, God had demonstrated his faithful commitment to his people. On many occasions, God had overlooked their disobedience and turning away from him and the paths he had laid out for them. But, as we see here and elsewhere, there does come a time when God will act and bring the judgment he warned about so that his people will be reminded of who he is and the jealous relationship he has for them.

And this idea, that the time is up, is made even clearer in the next chapter where God states explicitly that the end has come (Ezekiel 7:2). God is going to act in anger against his people, he is going to judge them based on how they have behaved, he is going to being them to account for the things they have continually done wrong (Ezekiel 7:3-4a). And, just as in the previous chapter, this judgment will result in the people being reminded again who God is and the relationship he has with them (Ezekiel 7:4b). If the relationship were not important, it might have been easier for God to let it go and to move on. But because of his commitment to them, because of the unending covenant with them, God acts in accordance with his promises in spite of the suffering it will cause. And we are left to wonder at how much it pained God to act against his people in this way, even as his anger could be contained no longer.

The impact of this is going to be felt through every level of society – with the king mourning, princes despairing, and the general population trembling before God as he acts in judgment against them. They all, whatever their position, will be clearly reminded of who God is (Ezekiel 7:27).

But while this was to impact everyone, there is extra warning for those in authority with a recognition that they have failed, they have led the people away, and so they are to face greater consequences. In Ezkiel 11, we see God singling out a group of the leaders of the people and accusing them of bringing evil and giving wicked advice against the city of Jerusalem (Ezekiel 11:2). They were even accused of killing many people in the city (Ezekiel 11:6). As a consequence, God is going to act against them, to drive them out, to send them into exile, to cause them to be killed (Ezekiel 11:8-10). Their crimes including not keeping God's laws but simply conforming to the standards of the surrounding nations and God was going to act to remind them of who he was (Ezekiel 11:11-12).

This idea is picked up again in the next chapter where God is speaking against the 'prince in Jerusalem and all who are there' (Ezekiel 12:10). Another period of exile is going to take place with more people being taken from Jerusalem to foreign lands. This is something God is going to do, in accordance with the warnings he gave centuries earlier, to remind them of who he is. And there is a slight message of hope as some of those sent away will recognise how much they have sinned against God and will turn back to him, acknowledging that he is their God (Ezekiel 12:15-16). But this will not stop this next part of the exile taking place leaving the towns destroyed and the land deserted – with the people recognising that God has acted as he said he would and that he, indeed, is faithful to who he has always been (Ezekiel 12:20).

It is not only the prince who is singled out for special warning and judgment, but the prophets of Israel who are speaking out of their own ideas as opposed to the word of God (Ezekiel 13:2). Because of their 'false words and lying visions' (Ezekiel 13:8), God is going to cast them out as though they have never been, reminding them of the God they have chosen to ignore (Ezekiel 13:9). The message of false peace they have spoken, the sense of false security they have built, will be revealed for what it is and will be brought down and God will be recognised as the only source of truth and safety (Ezekiel 13:13-14).

As well as the prophets, there are women who also prophesy from their own imagination (Ezekiel 13:17). They are accused of lying and only seeking their own gain and receive similar warnings of judgment and, as this judgment is carried out, they will also recognise the uniqueness of their God (Ezekiel 13:17-23).

And then there are elders who come to Ezekiel to seek God's word – but God makes clear to the prophet that these men are also following idols and so have lost the privilege of hearing God speaking to them (Ezekiel 14:1-3). God challenges them to turn away from those idols and their wicked practices and warns them that if they do come to him in that state he will answer but his answer will be to punish, to remove, to make them an example to others (Ezekiel 14:7-8), reminding the people of who God is.

The same message is given to the land, to the rulers, to the religious leaders and prophets. That because of their sin and their continual unwillingness to give God the honour and the place that he deserves, then God is going to act against them. And, as he does so, the things that they were trusting in, the things they were putting their confidence in, will not stand and they will be reminded – in ways they cannot ignore – that God is indeed the Lord, he is the one who has chosen them and called them to live in relationship with him.

This is made very clear in the eight verses of Ezekiel 15 which brings together the words of judgment and challenge into a simple, all encompassing, statement. The people have been unfaithful, they are no longer living as God called them to live, so God will act against them and – as he does – they will recognise, much too late, that God continues to be God and demands certain things of them due to the relationship he has called them into.

These warnings continue through Ezekiel 16-19 until, once again, in Ezekiel 20 we see God acting to remind his people of who he is. But here, God is reflecting on something that happened centuries earlier as the people God had rescued from Egypt persisted in not obeying him, not keeping his laws and not observing his Sabbaths (Ezekiel 20:21-22). This resulted in God warning them of exile, of adding laws that were impossible to keep and defiling them (Ezekiel 20:23-26). The language of these verses is difficult and the meaning is unclear[34] but what is clear is that this problem of disobedience, and God acting to remind them of who he is, had been there for hundreds of years. Ezekiel's point is that this behaviour was still continuing and so God was going to judge and act against them in the same way as before (Ezekiel 20:30-37). But while this will be difficult and painful, it is intended to root out those who are disobedient to God so that the people, as a whole, can return to him and know once again the relationship God wanted to have with them (Ezekiel 20:38).

---

[34] For a good discussion on this, see Daniel Isaac Block, *The Book of Ezekiel, Chapters 1–24*, The New International Commentary on the Old Testament (Grand Rapids, MI: Wm. B. Eerdmans Publishing Co., 1997), 636-641.

This will not just be something internal to the people of God, but something that will be recognised by the nations around them. Ezekiel 22:16 speaks about the people being 'defiled in the eyes of the nations', seemingly as a consequence of their exilic dispersal and God acting against them to as he removes their uncleanness from Jerusalem. As Block helpfully points out[35] this was something that God had warned them about before they entered the promised land. He had warned them that if they continued in idolatry they would be sent into exile where they would worship foreign gods (Deuteronomy 4:27) and that as a consequence of this they would be ridiculed by the nations (Deuteronomy 28:37). But, even then, there was a message of hope, an encouragement to turn back to God and to know him again (Deuteronomy 4:29-31). And Ezekiel makes this point again in verse 16 where he holds out hope that, even through all they experience, they will come back into relationship with their God who had never abandoned them.

Ezekiel reinforces this idea in Ezekiel 23:49 where he restates the fact that the people will suffer for their idolatry, they will reap the consequences, and that – through that – they will come to recognise the sovereignty of God once again.

Even the destruction of Jerusalem did not change how the remaining people thought (Ezekiel 33:21-22). Those who were left to scratch out a living in the ruins of their city had a mistaken belief that the promise of the land continued to apply to them, even though they persisted in living in idolatry and disobedience to God's laws. But God calls on Ezekiel to speak against this, to make it clear that further judgment will come, and the land will be laid waste in response to the sinful ways God's people have been living. And, at that point, the people will once again recognise who God is, and the relationship he had called them into which they had neglected and spurned.

---

[35] Daniel Isaac Block, *The Book of Ezekiel, Chapters 1–24*, The New International Commentary on the Old Testament (Grand Rapids, MI: Wm. B. Eerdmans Publishing Co., 1997), 713.

God acts against Ezekiel as a sign to the people

There is one further passage we are going to look at where God acts to remind his people that he is their God, that he is Lord. It is in Ezekiel 24:15-27 which is a very sad, and shocking, section of the book where God warns Ezekiel that his wife is going to die. In fact, that God was going to take "the delight of your eyes" away from him (Ezekiel 24:16). This is one of the most difficult passages in this challenging book as we are left to wonder how this could be right, how this relates to our understanding of God.

The point given here is clear – that it was going to be a sign to the people to whom Ezekiel was prophesying. It would have been expected, in the custom of his day, for him to perform various mourning rituals but God expressly forbade him to do so. This would have been clearly visible to the people around him, and so unexpected that they would have wanted to know why he was behaving like that. And he is to tell them that God is going to act in a similar way to take away the "delight of their eyes" – referring to the destruction of the temple in Jerusalem and their sons and daughters who remained in Jerusalem coming to join them in exile. And this was to be such a tragic event, would affect them so significantly, that normal mourning rituals would not be enough to deal with their grief, they would not know how to respond and their sorrow would eat away at them.

As they hear news of this happening, in accordance with the prophetic sign and words of Ezekiel, the people would recognise that this further destruction and additional exile was not a random act but directly under the control of God. And they would recognise again that he was God, that he was Sovereign, that he was Lord.

A powerful symbol that must have really spoken to the people – and would maybe have caused some to turn away from their idolatry and back to God. But it was too late for the temple and too late for those still in Jerusalem. And it was too late for Ezekiel's wife.

Which takes us back to our question of why God chose to act in this way.

It's worth recognising that, from the moment he was called to act as God's prophet, Ezekiel had suffered in a number of ways to be a sign to the people. His calling was not just to speak but to act as directed by God to reinforce the power and impact of his words.

At the beginning of his ministry, God warned Ezekiel about some of the things that were going to happen: he was going to be tied up; God was going to take his voice away from him so that he could not speak to the people unless God had given him a specific prophetic word to deliver (Ezekiel 3:25-27).

He was commanded to act out the siege of Jerusalem by building a model of it and lying on his side next to it for a total of 430 days, and to live on a very poor diet of bread and water while he was doing it. A symbol of the siege of Jerusalem and the lack of food and water those living there would experience (Ezekiel 4).

He was instructed to shave the hair of his head and beard (which would have resulted in great shame) and to burn, strike and scatter the hair as a sign of the suffering and scattering that would come on the people in Jerusalem (Ezekiel 5:1-4).

He was told to act out the impending further exile by packing his bags, making a hole in the wall and escaping through it, just as people in Jerusalem would do as they tried, but failed, to escape the surrounding forces (Ezekiel 12:1-14).

He was to groan in front of the people as a prediction of the grief that would consume them as Jerusalem was destroyed (Ezekiel 21:5-7).

He was to act out the decision that the king of Babylon would take as he tried to determine whether he would attack the people of Ammon or the people of Jerusalem, and to make clear that it was Jerusalem that would be attacked and fall (Ezekiel 21:18-24).

Ezekiel had suffered much as he was faithful to the prophetic call of God on his life, and he is not the only one of those who have done much for God who have been called to suffer. God made it clear to Paul that his ministry was going to include much suffering (Acts 9:16), Hebrews 11:35-38 lists some of those who suffered as a result of their allegiance to God, Jesus made it clear that following him would involve suffering (Matthew 16:24), Jesus himself suffered above all others at the hands of his people and on the cross (Matthew 16:21, Luke 24:46, Hebrews 2:9). So it is something that "comes with the territory" and something we should expect if we are serious about following the call of Jesus on our lives. But it is still difficult to see the way in which Ezekiel's wife was used to provide a sign of what God was going to do in Jerusalem.

It's worth considering why this is so difficult to accept in the context of a book which has many occasions where God speaks about bringing death and destruction on his people in response to their persistently sinful lifestyle. Why should the death of this one woman stand out? There are at least two reasons: it is often more difficult to think of what is happening to a named individual than to larger, more anonymous, groups; we have no reason to believe she is particularly guilty of the things that Ezekiel has been speaking against, on the contrary she was probably a support and encouragement to him in all that he was enduring for God as a result of his calling.

Cooper recognises this when he asks 'Did God commit an unprovoked act of cruelty in taking the life of Ezekiel's wife, who was called "the delight" of his eyes (v. 16), just to illustrate a point?'[36] He thinks that Ezekiel's wife probably contracted a sudden and fatal disease and argues that:

God would not arbitrarily take the life of Ezekiel's wife to clarify his word to an unrepentant people. But he would speak in the midst of the inevitable suffering of life to show them that he knows, he cares, and he will use the suffering as a basis for a hope of new life.[37]

---

[36] Lamar Eugene Cooper, *Ezekiel*, vol. 17, The New American Commentary (Nashville: Broadman & Holman Publishers, 1994), 238.
[37] Lamar Eugene Cooper, *Ezekiel*, vol. 17, The New American Commentary (Nashville: Broadman & Holman Publishers, 1994), 238.

Wright recognizes the challenge of this passage but does not think we can soften the blow by assuming Ezekiel's wife suffered a natural illness. He says:

The Bible makes no secret of the cost involved in being a servant of God in a hostile world, and many faithful prophets suffered in the course of their ministry, including suffering in the intimacy of their personal lives. But the death of a young wife seems outrageously cruel. It does not seem that we can take refuge in imagining that it was a natural illness and death which was later interpreted by Ezekiel in this way. His account is too specific for that. Yahweh took his wife—with a warning, yes, but still it was Yahweh's direct action that left him desolate. We need to set this fact alongside what we know of God from 18:32 and 33:11. If God takes no pleasure in the death of anyone, even the wicked, then how much more was it an act of 'no pleasure', but rather of terrible grief, for God to take the life of this presumably believing and righteous young woman?[38]

And he goes on to make the point that this looks forward to the time when God will give up his own Son as a means of restoring his kingdom:

But he is not alone among those who have lost loved ones in the service of the word of God, and whose loss has borne mysterious fruit in the salvation of others. Nor was Ezekiel alone in paying the cost of the death of his most dearly beloved for the sake of others. His pain was in some mysterious sense a sharing in the pain of God. For the God who took Ezekiel's wife was the God who would give up his own beloved Son to death on the cross. And he did so because he so loved the world, including the exiles who crowded Ezekiel's desolate home that day. If any of those exiles are among the saved whom we shall meet in the new creation, it will ultimately be because of Christ's sacrifice, not Ezekiel's.[39]

---

[38] Christopher J. H. Wright, *The Message of Ezekiel: A New Heart and a New Spirit*, ed. Alec Motyer and Derek Tidball, The Bible Speaks Today (Nottingham, England: Inter-Varsity Press, 2001), 218.

[39] Christopher J. H. Wright, *The Message of Ezekiel: A New Heart and a New Spirit*, ed. Alec Motyer and Derek Tidball, The Bible Speaks Today (Nottingham, England: Inter-Varsity Press, 2001), 218.

Friebel argues, however, that her death was not something God caused intentionally but was something subsequently used by Ezekiel to communicate his message:

> The occurrence of the death of Ezekiel's wife was not an intentional action performed by Ezekiel, as rhetor, nor intentionally designed to communicate a message-content. The manner of expression in v. 16 that God was going 'to take' Ezekiel's wife must not be understood in the sense that God caused her death intentionally for the purpose of providing Ezekiel with an opportunity to communicate a prophetic message. Her death is analogous to Saul tearing Samuel's robe (1 Sam. 15:27–28) and the potter remaking the marred vessel (Jer. 18). Neither Saul nor the potter performed the actions intentionally to communicate messages or to provide the occasions for prophetic messages, yet the actions became appropriate events which the prophets, subsequent to the actions, intentionally encoded with message-contents. So too Ezekiel's wife's death was antecedent to the communication event, but was subsequently encoded with communicative meaning. The event was used like an 'artifact' which provided the proper setting and timing for the reactive behaviors intentionally performed by Ezekiel which bore the primary message-content.[40]

Whatever we conclude actually happened here, there is a feeling of real sadness as we are allowed to share in a deeply personal and painful experience in the life of the prophet and encouraged to wonder whether even this powerful sign had any impact on the people around him. Or were they so far away from an appreciation of God and what he required of them, that even this would only have a momentary impact with no real change occurring? Or would this break through to some people and cause them to turn away from idolatry and return to their God?

---

[40] Kelvin G. Friebel, *Jeremiah's and Ezekiel's Sign-Acts*, vol. 283, Journal for the Study of the Old Testament Supplement Series (Sheffield: Sheffield Academic Press, 1999), 336–337.

Implications for us

So far in this book, we've looked at different stories from the book of Ezekiel and used them to get an understanding of what was going on, how his people's behaviour grieved God greatly and caused him to act and – most importantly – seen something of the value that God places on the honour of his name and the lengths he will go to in order to defend it. As we have done so, it has become clear that God's primary motive for action may not always be about what would make things better or easier for his people but what would demonstrate his glory.

This might be a new thought, it might be a challenging idea, it might cause us to re-evaluate our understanding of God. But if we recognise the reality of it, then the story told by Ezekiel has some difficult and challenging questions for those of us who pray for God's name to be honoured. We have looked at some of these earlier, but in this last chapter we are going to pull those ideas together and summarise what this might mean for how we think, what we say and what we do. If we want to live in a way that honours God's name – not just pray that it will happen and then do what we want to please ourselves.

The problem of idolatry

We started by looking at the problem of idolatry among the people of God, something that God had made totally clear that it was unacceptable to him. We saw that it had been going on for a long time, since before God rescued them from Egypt. And even though God did bring them out, this was nothing to do with whether they deserved it but all about God honouring his name through keeping his promises. We saw that idolatry continued through their wilderness journey and into the Promised Land, that it was very present during the time of the Judges, it was even continued through the lives of some of their kings. It was still true in the time of Ezekiel, appearing in a number of different ways: erecting idols in the place where God alone should be worshipped, leaders of the people engaging in secret idolatry, people crying out to false gods seeking their blessing and help, people putting created objects above their creator. Centuries earlier, God had warned his people that if they behaved in this way, he would punish them; now he restates these warnings reminding us that punishment delayed does not mean that punishment has been avoided.

We also saw that one of the ways in which this problem appeared was with the people allowing the things they owned to become their idols, just as they had in the incident of the golden calf and Gideon making an ephod.

And their story raises challenges for us today.

One of the ideas behind God's name being recognised as holy is that we acknowledge that God is "other", that he is unique, that there is no one else and nothing else that compares to him. As soon as we step away from that and engage in any type of idolatrous practices, then we are saying that the place God alone deserves is to be shared with someone or something else. This means that we are no longer treating God's name as holy. So, allowing any form of idolatry in our lives is totally inconsistent with us praying that God's name be seen as holy. This was the mistake that the people of God fell into centuries ago, and a mistake we should seek to avoid making today.

When we pray for God's name to be honoured, and it is important that we do, are we living lives that seek to honour him or are we putting something else or someone else in God's place? Are we focused on him or are we more focused on what we have and what that can do for us? Are we turning our possessions into idols as opposed to giving God the worship and first place that he deserves?

- As I pray these words, am I allowing anyone or anything else to take the place that God alone deserves?
- As I pray these words, am I acting in such a way that would cause others to not give God the honour he deserves?
- As I pray these words, am I allowing my position or possessions to take the place that God demands in my life?

Consequences of disobedience

In the second chapter, we looked at the reality that disobedience carries consequences. The people were deeply privileged to have been chosen by God and they are repaying it by turning away and breaking the laws that God had given them. God's response is clear – he is against them and was going to punish them, He saw himself as their enemy and would treat them as such. As he does so, the surrounding nations will see and be reminded of the danger of going against God.

And the prospect of God choosing to do similar things today, in response to ongoing disobedience of his people, is very real.

When we pray - as per the Lord's prayer - for God's name to be honoured, we need to recognise that our actions and behaviours can be the cause of God's name being honoured or dishonoured. We don't just pray about it, our actions have an impact on it.

At the time of writing, there seems to have been a succession of high-profile Christian leaders exposed for acts of various forms of abuse. Recent research has also shown that this is present in some of our churches where, often, much is done to cover things up.[41] As well as the deep harm this brings to victims of such abuse, these actions bring the church into disrepute and dishonours the name of God.

---

[41] See, for example, Lisa Oakley and Justin Humphreys, *Escaping the Maze of*

Sometimes our churches become places where we are more focused on what we enjoy than on what God wants and gives glory to him.

Many of us will know fellow believers whose lives fall far short of the example of Jesus. As we examine ourselves, we will probably see areas where we are not living as he calls us to live.

Are we relying on God's grace and the hope that he will continue to allow these things to happen? Should we be concerned that God will come and act in judgment against us?

Jesus speaks words of warning to churches in Revelation:

- He challenges the church at Pergamum about allowing false teaching and warns that, unless they repent, he will come and fight against them (Revelation 2:14-16)
- He challenges the church at Thyatira about tolerating acts of immorality and warns against bringing suffering upon them so other churches will see and know that God judges (Revelation 2:20-23)
- For the church at Sardis, his warning is about having gone to sleep on the job, of failing to carry out the commission he has given them (Revelation 3:1-2)
- He warns the church at Laodicea that due to their half-heartedness and lack of awareness of the reality of their situation he may come and get rid of them (Revelation 3:15-16)

Ezekiel shows us that God was prepared to act against his people who had dishonoured his name; Revelation warns us that Jesus is prepared to do the same against his churches who do not live as his people are called to live.

As we pray for God's name to be honoured, let us also recommit ourselves to acting in a way that honours the name of our God, that brings glory to Jesus. And for this to be seen powerfully and clearly by the people around us.

Spiritual Abuse: Creating Healthy Christian Cultures (London: SPCK, 2019)

Leaders going astray

The third chapter brought a specific focus on the problems of leaders turning away from God and his purposes – and then taking the people they led with them. This included those who were in positions of civil authority, those who were religious leaders, those who were responsible for speaking God's word to the people. They were no longer focusing on God, "remembering him", obeying his laws, or living up to what was expected of them. Rather they were taking advantage of their position and exploiting those they should have been leading, guiding, teaching, and providing for.

We saw that, as a consequence, this type of behaviour had spread to everyone in the land as they followed the examples of their leaders. A shocking state of affairs – one that certainly did not preserve the honour of God's name.

And it's not a problem that was confined to people in the Old Testament, it was still there in the early church:

Evidently some people are throwing you into confusion and are trying to pervert the gospel of Christ. (Galatians 1:7)

I wrote to the church, but Diotrephes, who loves to be first, will not welcome us. So when I come, I will call attention to what he is doing, spreading malicious nonsense about us. Not satisfied with that, he even refuses to welcome other believers. He also stops those who want to do so and puts them out of the church. (3 John 9–10)

And, sadly, it is easy to look at different parts of society and the church and to see examples of this happening today.

We see people in positions of authority in all walks of life – politics, the media, businesses, churches, charities – exploiting their status and using it for their own purposes. This can result in the needy not being provided for, the poor not being supported, the outcast not being welcomed, family relationships breaking down, unhealthy business practices being encouraged, the vulnerable being abused and more.

We are not 'princes of Israel'[42] but many of us will have influence and authority in some areas of our lives. Maybe in our families, in our jobs, in our neighbourhoods, in our churches. It is important to regularly examine ourselves to see whether we are 'remembering God' – acknowledging him, being obedient to him, seeking to serve and bless others – or whether we have 'forgotten God' – taking advantage of our position and exploiting those for whom we have responsibility. It is only from a position of 'remembering God' and the implications of that, that we can really pray that God's name be honoured.

Within our churches these positions of authority can be many and various: pastors, priests, ministers; trustees, deacons, elders; administrators, secretaries; worship group leaders, small group leaders, leaders of activities for children and young people; the list goes on.

Each of these people and groups have a responsibility to grow in their relationship with God, to recognise the privileged position they have been given, to seek to understand and be obedient to God's plans and purposes for their areas of responsibility, to be a blessing and encouragement to those among whom they minister and serve.

Are we still looking for godly character in the lives of those we seek out as leaders – the sort of characteristics that Paul describes when writing about elders and deacons in 1 Timothy 3:1-13? People who are "above reproach", "worthy of respect", keeping "hold of the deep truths of the faith", having "a good reputation with outsiders", "sincere" and much more.

If our leaders do not have such characteristics, if they are not passionate for God and seeking to honour him in all they do then the church will become a place where God's name is not honoured, however much we pray for it to be so as we recite the words of the Lord's prayer.

---

[42] at least that's the case for most of us reading this book!

Defending the honour of God's name

In the bridging chapter, we recognised that these things only really mattered if God cared that his people had turned against him and were bringing dishonour on his name. And Ezekiel makes totally clear that God is passionately concerned about defending the honour of his name and will act strongly and decisively to do so.

- He brought this idolatrous people out of Egypt to defend the honour of his name
- He kept back from destroying them to defend the honour of his name
- He had sent them into exile to defend the honour of his name
- He was going to bring them back from exile to defend the honour of his name
- He acted so that the nations around him would recognise the honour of his name
- He was going to defeat mighty armies to demonstrate the power of his name
- He was going to return to the abandoned temple so that his name could, once again, be honoured

Time and time again, the book of Ezekiel makes it totally clear that God will act to restore and to defend the honour of his name – and will act against his own wayward people as well as opposing nations in order to do so.

Observers watching the land of Israel and the people of God in the time around the exile would have seen many things and, potentially, have come up with many reasons for them.

As the people of the land turned away from God and went further and further into idolatry, these observers could easily have concluded that they had given up on God and were seeking their own way to live. And as the years went by, it would have been easy to assume that God either could not do anything about it or didn't care enough to act, that God had given up on them.

And as the events of the exile started to unfold, it would have been easy to think that this was happening as God was unable to keep his people safe and that other nations, with their gods, had been demonstrated to be more powerful.

As the exiles started to return, our observers could have asked questions about the lenience of the foreign rulers and how the people were going to live once again in their land. Would they continue as they had previously, or would their experiences have changed them forever?

And as they looked towards the East and saw God's glory coming back and settling on the Temple, would all of their carefully developed ideas come tumbling down as they recognised that God was still there and, in some way, he was back with his people?

God's perspective, the only one that matters, is that all these things took place to defend the honour of his name.

In one of the first recorded persecutions in the early church, the apostles had just been flogged and ordered to not speak any more in the name of Jesus. Their response was powerful:

"The apostles left the Sanhedrin, rejoicing because they had been counted worthy of suffering disgrace for the Name." (Acts 5:41)

For them, the thing that was important was that they were living, speaking, breathing to being honour to the name of Jesus – and were even willing to suffer their own personal disgrace to do so.

When we look at what is going on around us: in our lives, in our families, in our churches – what do we see, what lens do we use? Are we looking at things from our own perspectives or are we seeking to see how our actions and behaviour may affect the honour of God's name? Do we think about what God might continue to choose to do in order to defend it?

The God of glory

We spent time looking at the topic of the glory of God – his majesty, his power, the things he has done. We saw how this glory was seen in the Old Testament – particularly in the places where God chose to come and meet with his people, we saw how it was demonstrated perfectly in Jesus and we also saw how it was a recurring theme in Ezekiel.

God's glorious appearance was seen in a strange and powerful vision at the beginning of the book, God's glory was seen by Ezekiel in another vision even while acts of idolatry were going on around him, we see God's glory leaving the temple and the city in a powerful symbol that God was leaving his people, we see God choosing to act to demonstrate his glory among the surrounding nations, we see God's glory returning to inhabit the temple again. God did these various things in response to the attitudes, behaviours and actions of his people. While his glory cannot be taken away from him, he can choose to remove it from his people if they continue to turn away from him.

God's glory is an indication of his presence, but it does not depend on his people or anyone else – it is something that is intrinsic to God's character and can never be taken from him. But the challenge for God's people, then and now, is whether they are going to live in such a way that they can continue to enjoy the presence of God's glory or whether they are going to turn so far away from God that he acts in judgment against them again.

As we pray for God's name to be honoured, we are aligning ourselves with God's purpose – and it is important that our actions align in the same way as well.

God as "the Lord"

In the previous chapter, we were reminded of the lordship of God – a title that speaks about the relationship God has with his chosen people, and often demonstrated in the powerful ways he had acted on their behalf in the past. And that, even in the midst of everything that was going on that caused God deep sorrow, this relationship had not changed. He was still their God, they were still his people. But, instead of the actions he was going to take being for their good, they were going to result in devastation for the people as God acts in accordance with his promises to them. He did this so that they would know him for who he was and he was even prepared to put his prophet Ezekiel into difficult and deeply distressing situations to act as a sign to the people. Being the people of God can result in very distressing things happening if those people continually and consistently turn against their God and cause distress and dishonour to him.

As we have explored some of the lengths God was prepared and willing to go to in order to remind his people of their relationship with him, to remind them that he was their God, we have been made painfully aware that the fact of being in relationship with God does not protect his people from his acts of judgment against them. Acts that are designed to restore and to rekindle an awareness of the greatness and sovereignty of God but acts that are painful and distressing for the wayward people of God.

One of the things we saw is that, even during the exile the people still in Jerusalem were resting in "possessing the land" and thinking that ensured their safety. God, through his prophet, pointed out that this was not the case, and that judgment would fall on them as well. They were living in the place that God had given them, things seemed to be ok, and they assumed that this would continue. And this can be something we can slip into as we continue in our churches that have, often, been established and continued for so long.

Because one of the ways that those who believe in God can often think is that when times are going well it is because God is blessing them, and when things are hard they are out of God's favour who is punishing them. And there is certainly biblical evidence to support the view that God will bless those who align themselves to him.

As they were about to enter the Promised Land, God promised to bless his people if they were obedient to him:

However, there need be no poor people among you, for in the land the LORD your God is giving you to possess as your inheritance, he will richly bless you, if only you fully obey the LORD your God and are careful to follow all these commands I am giving you today. (Deuteronomy 15:4–5)

In Isaiah 58, the prophet is challenging the people about fasting and telling them that if they behave in particular ways, then they will experience God's blessing:

- If they oppose injustice, free the oppressed, feed the hungry, provide shelter for those on a journey, clothe the naked and care for their family – then they themselves will shine brightly, be healed and be protected by God's glory, they will call out to God and he will answer, they will cry out for help and he will provide it (Is 58:8-9)
- If they get rid of oppressive burdens, turn away from accusations and gossip, devote themselves to helping the hungry and oppressed – then there will be light over all they do, God will guide them, he will give them all they need (Is 58:9-11)
- If they observe the Sabbath and delight in honouring God on the day he has set aside, don't engage in idle talk – then they will rejoice in God and live triumphantly (Is 58:13-14)

Psalm 112 has phrase after phrase that speaks about the blessings that will flow to those who fear God, treat people well and act justly. For such people:

- Their children will do well and be strong, that generation will be blessed (Ps 112:2)
- They will enjoy riches and wealth and a good name (Ps 112:3)
- They will live in the light even when times are hard (Ps 112:4)
- They will rejoice in good things (Ps 112:5)
- They will not be shaken and will leave behind good reputations (Ps 112:6)
- They are not troubled by bad news because they are confidently trusting in God and feel totally secure (Ps 112:8)

- They will be honoured while the wicked will fail and be jealous (Ps 112:10)

So there is a clear thread throughout scripture that God blesses those who are seeking him, honouring him and living for him. And this may lead to the view that if things are going well, then we are experiencing God's blessing and so we are living in a way that is pleasing to him.

But, while that may be true on occasions, the story of Ezekiel makes clear that this is not necessarily the case. Ezekiel shows that it is possible, at least for a time, to experience rich blessings even if the way people are behaving is totally opposed to and dishonouring to God. Are we resting in the idea that God doesn't really mind what we do so long as we continue to keep our churches open, or do we recognise that God is looking for people who live to honour his name? This is some of what it means to recognise that Jesus is Lord. We may be experiencing blessing in our churches, we may be seeing growth in our ministries, but are we really living to bring honour to the name of Jesus?

Reflecting again on the words of Jesus to the church at Sardis show us that the danger can be very real:

- A church or ministry may well have a reputation of being faithful, of doing good things, of moving forward God's kingdom (Rev 3:1)
- But Jesus can look at it and declare them as "unfinished", and requiring repentance (Rev 3:2-3)
- And that if the church does not respond, Jesus will come against it in judgment (Rev 3:3)

Living the prayer

And so we get back to where we started!

We may regularly pray that God's name is to be hallowed, to be kept holy, to be honoured. As we do so we are publicly calling for God's kingdom to become more present on this earth than it currently is.

But if our lives are not aligned with that desire, that purpose and – instead – allowing other things to take the place that God alone should have then our words are hollow and we are placing ourselves in a dangerous position.

Let's pray it, but let's also live to make it a reality - not allowing anything to creep in that would draw us away from God and his plans and purposes.

Consecrate yourselves and be holy, because I am the LORD your God. Keep my decrees and follow them. I am the LORD, who makes you holy. (Leviticus 20:7–8)

Finally, brothers and sisters, whatever is true, whatever is noble, whatever is right, whatever is pure, whatever is lovely, whatever is admirable—if anything is excellent or praiseworthy—think about such things. (Philippians 4:8)

Bibliography

Bibles

NET, *The NET Bible First Edition; Bible. English. NET Bible.; The NET Bible* (Biblical Studies Press, 2005)

NIV, *The New International Version* (Grand Rapids, MI: Zondervan, 2011)

NLT, *Holy Bible: New Living Translation* (Carol Stream, IL: Tyndale House Publishers, 2015)

Other Books

Archer Jr., Gleason, *A Survey of Old Testament Introduction, 3rd. ed.* (Chicago: Moody Press, 1994)

Bernard, D. T., *"Ezekiel on the Early History of Religion in Israel.—Ch. 20," The Churchman 17, no. 1–12* (1902–1903)

Block, Daniel Isaac, *The Book of Ezekiel, Chapters 1–24,* The New International Commentary on the Old Testament (Grand Rapids, MI: Wm. B. Eerdmans Publishing Co., 1997)

Block, Daniel Isaac, *The Book of Ezekiel, Chapters 25–48,* The New International Commentary on the Old Testament (Grand Rapids, MI: Wm. B. Eerdmans Publishing Co., 1997–)

Blomberg, Craig, *Matthew,* vol. 22, The New American Commentary (Nashville: Broadman & Holman Publishers, 1992)

Carson, D. A., *"Matthew,"* in The Expositor's Bible Commentary: Matthew, Mark, Luke, ed. Frank E. Gaebelein, vol. 8 (Grand Rapids, MI: Zondervan Publishing House, 1984)

Cooper, Lamar Eugene, *Ezekiel,* vol. 17, The New American Commentary (Nashville: Broadman & Holman Publishers, 1994)

France, R. T., *The Gospel of Matthew,* The New International Commentary on the New Testament (Grand Rapids, MI: Wm. B. Eerdmans Publication Co., 2007)

Friebel, Kelvin G., *Jeremiah's and Ezekiel's Sign-Acts,* vol. 283, Journal for the Study of the Old Testament Supplement Series (Sheffield: Sheffield Academic Press, 1999)

Greenberg, Moshe, *Ezekiel 1–20: A New Translation with Introduction and Commentary,* vol. 22, Anchor Yale Bible (New Haven; London: Yale University Press, 2008)

Harrington, Daniel J., "Antiochus," ed. David Noel Freedman, Allen C. Myers, and Astrid B. Beck, *Eerdmans Dictionary of the Bible* (Grand Rapids, MI: W.B. Eerdmans, 2000)

Koester, Craig R., *Hebrews: A New Translation with Introduction and Commentary,* vol. 36, Anchor Yale Bible (New Haven; London: Yale University Press, 2008)

MacArthur, John and Richard Mayhue, eds., *Biblical Doctrine: A Systematic Summary of Bible Truth* (Wheaton, IL: Crossway, 2017)

Merriam-Webster, Inc, *Merriam-Webster's Collegiate Dictionary.* (Springfield, MA: Merriam-Webster, Inc., 2003).

Morris, Leon, *The Gospel according to Matthew,* The Pillar New Testament Commentary (Grand Rapids, MI; Leicester, England: W.B. Eerdmans; Inter-Varsity Press, 1992)

Oakley, Lisa and Justin Humphreys, *Escaping the Maze of Spiritual Abuse: Creating Healthy Christian Cultures* (London: SPCK, 2019)

O'Brien, Peter T., *The Letter to the Hebrews,* The Pillar New Testament Commentary (Grand Rapids, MI; Nottingham, England: William B. Eerdmans Publishing Company, 2010)

Smith, Ralph L., *Micah–Malachi,* vol. 32, Word Biblical Commentary (Dallas: Word, Incorporated, 1984)

Thompson, J. A., *Deuteronomy: An Introduction and Commentary,* vol. 5, Tyndale Old Testament Commentaries (Downers Grove, IL: InterVarsity Press, 1974)

Wright, Christopher J. H., *The Message of Ezekiel: A New Heart and a New Spirit,* ed. Alec Motyer and Derek Tidball, The Bible Speaks Today (Nottingham, England: Inter-Varsity Press, 2001)

Wright, Tom, *Matthew for Everyone, Part 1: Chapters 1-15* (London: Society for Promoting Christian Knowledge, 2004)

Printed in Great Britain
by Amazon